D0230567

Mick Wall is the UK's best-known rock writer and broadcaster, and is the author of numerous critically acclaimed books, including definitive, bestselling titles on Led Zeppelin (*When Giants Walked the Earth*), Metallica (*Enter Night*), AC/DC (*Hell Ain't a Bad Place to Be*) and Black Sabbath (*Symptom of the Universe*). He lives in England.

By Mick Wall

Lou Reed: The Life

Black Sabbath: Symptom of the Universe

AC/DC: Hell Ain't a Bad Place to Be

Enter Night: Metallica – The Biography

Appetite for Destruction

When Giants Walked the Earth – A Biography of Led Zeppelin

W.A.R.: The Unauthorised Biography of W. Axl Rose

Bono – In the Name of Love

John Peel – A Tribute to the Much-Loved DJ and Broadcaster

XS All Areas: The Autobiography of Status Quo

Mr Big: Ozzy and my Life as the Godfather of Rock by Don Arden

Paranoid: Black Days with Sabbath & Other Horror Stories

Run to the Hills: The Authorised Biography of Iron Maiden

Pearl Jam

Guns N' Roses: The Most Dangerous Band in the World

Diary of a Madman – The Official Biography of Ozzy Osbourne

LOU REED
The Life

MICK WALL

An Orion paperback

First published in Great Britain in 2013 by Orion
This paperback edition published in 2014
by Orion Books Ltd,
Orion House, 5 Upper St Martin's Lane,
London WC2H 9EA

An Hachette UK company

10 9 8 7 6 5 4 3 2

A CIP catalogue record for this book is available
from the British Library.

ISBN 978-1-4091-5304-7

Printed and bound in Great Britain by CPI Group (UK),
Croydon CR0 4YY

The Orion Publishing Group's policy is to use papers
that are natural, renewable and recyclable products and
made from wood grown in sustainable forests. The logging
and manufacturing processes are expected to conform to
the environmental regulations of the country of origin.

www.orionbooks.co.uk

This book is dedicated to:

LINDA WALL
ROBERT KIRBY
JANE STURROCK
MALCOLM EDWARDS
VANESSA LAMPERT
HARRY PATERSON
DEE HEMBURY-EATON
& MICK BEVAN

I would also like to thank the following people: Lisa Milton, Emma Smith, Kate Wright-Morris, Kirsty Howarth, Mark Handsley, Susan Howe, Jessica Purdue, Helen Ewing, Craig Fraser, Holly Thomson, Colin and Diana Cartwright, and Ian Ross.

Preface: The Long Night   xiii

1 ECT   1

2 Flowers Of Evil   25

3 Light And Dark   51

4 Unloaded   71

5 Breakup To Makeup   93

6 Suicide City   119

7 White Noise   143

8 Hey, Shut Up!   159

9 The New Mask   177

10 The Tao of Lou Reed   195

Discography   215

Notes and Sources   231

'An artist is an artist only because of his exquisite sense of beauty, a sense which shows him intoxicating pleasures, but which at the same time implies and contains an equally exquisite sense of all deformities, and all disproportion.'

Charles Baudelaire

Preface: The Long Night

Perhaps the greatest gift Lou Reed bequeathed his audience was that he never stopped writing songs about drugs, squalor, transgressive sexuality, and characters with wonderful names like Lulu, Sister Ray, Candy Darling and Newspaper Joe. About honourable prostitutes, visionary gutter queens, and their photo-negatives, the holy roller pimps and dollar-hustlers, the two-way sailors and bad connections who plied their trade not on just the streets of Lou's beloved New York but in the multi-storey boardrooms, newspaper offices and TV studios that looked down on them, the ones who brayed loudest about being right in a world gone wrong. The real fixers who got their contact-highs not from tying up their arms and sliding in a needle, but from knowing which switches to throw, the ones that controlled all our lives, in a kind of permanent midnight that never quite reaches dawn, new, or otherwise indisposed.

Lou Reed may have got sober over the years – and good for us he did: the guy with the translucent, skull-like features and swastikas shaved into the side of his head whose 'girlfriend' was a bearded he-she named Rachel, the speed freak who would stay up for five days and who knew as much about the intricacies of human pharmacology as he did the algorithms of recording technology, would simply not have survived the 1970s otherwise, let alone made it upright to the next century – but he never became 'an earnest AIDS crusader or a celebrity supporter of Barack Obama', as the late, great *Sunday Times* critic Robert Sandall so memorably put it. You never found Lou glad-handing it on the *Jonathan Ross Show* or showing up to crack wise on *America's Got Talent*.

No. The man whom his own record company used to call 'The Phantom of Rock', whose nihilistic, depressed, suicidal, transgender, piss-taking mission statements caused endless 'offence', never truly disgraced himself by moving like Jagger into a self-denying rock netherworld where he became the most skeletal jukebox in town. 'I do Lou Reed better than anybody,' Lou famously said, and it was true. But he never let us all down by feeling the need to prove it year after year like the ageless – she wishes – Madonna.

Instead, Lou Reed was the famous singer who had hardly any hits, but remained not just the voice of the repressed and downtrodden, the miserable and driven insane, but the guy who actually knew where all the bodies were buried and was happy to point them out whether anybody asked him to or not. He had, after all, helped put a few of them there himself over the years, and a nasty spectacle it was too, watching him turn his back on Cale and Nico, like his first wife Bettye and second-best girlfriend Bowie, even in the end Andy Warhol, who raised him like one of his own, only to be repaid with a vicious slap in the kisser. Vicious, you know, like hit me with a flower. That had been Andy's idea too but so what? You think these people didn't shit on Lou Reed too?

From the very first album he ever made, *The Velvet Underground & Nico*, in 1967, dismissed at the time as, at best, the work of one of Andy Warhol's less interesting Factory freaks, at worst as an offensive and entirely inappropriate misreading of the prevailing love-is-all-you-need zeitgeist; to *Metal Machine Music*, utterly ridiculed upon its release in 1975, despite later becoming the template for such art-punk terrorists as Throbbing Gristle and, most recently, the avant-garde German string ensemble Zeitkratzer; right up to the last ever album he would release in his lifetime, his much disparaged collaboration with Metallica, *Lulu*, in 2011, the endlessly ridiculed winner of every Worst Ever list since – nothing Lou Reed ever did was fully embraced first time around.

It was the same even with his greatest commercial success, *Transformer*, in 1972. The great Charles Shaar Murray described it in his *NME* review as 'too slight, too trivial, too lightweight to live up to… the Velvets'. The same week, in his column for *Disc And Music Echo*, the even greater John Peel described 'Walk On The Wild Side' as 'depressing'. But then if you'd told Lou Reed back then that one day 'Perfect Day', his perfect love song about two junkies spending a day in the park trying to forget who they are, would years later become a children's charity single, on which the great and the good of the pop world, from Bono to Tom Jones, would line up impatiently just to sing a line, sending it to No. 1, he'd have probably stabbed you in the eye with his syringe.

For me there was never any doubt about who Lou Reed was or what it was he was doing with his music, even as a 14-year-old in 1973 who hadn't begun shaving his face yet, let alone his legs. Of course, I didn't get any of the Warhol in-jokes on *Transformer*, but I sure felt the closeness of the heat that songs like 'Walk On The Wild Side' gave off. It was *Berlin*, though, released later the same year, that really did it for me. Like reading *Naked Lunch* for the first time, or sneaking in to see *A Clockwork Orange* before they yanked it from the cinemas, again I was overwhelmed by the detail, but left in no doubt whatsoever about the feelings those bitter, beautiful, terrible songs stirred in my suddenly not-so-young-any-more soul.

I had no idea, though, that I would spend the rest of my life periodically trying to *explain* Lou Reed to people, even others who got the Velvet Underground, could dig *Transformer* and *Berlin* and even parts of *Coney Island Baby* but just shrugged and switched off whenever I was foolish enough to bring up *The Blue Mask*, or even *New York*, and, God forbid, *Lulu*. (Still, for me, one of the great unsung rock'n'roll masterpieces of the century but which *Classic Rock* magazine made me rewrite my review of, insisting I 'tone it down' as everyone else in the office considered it basically unlistenable to.)

And I feel exceedingly foolish right now for even bothering; writing these words and seeing how they make me look. It's not like Lou Reed didn't release more than his fair share of stinkers. But then so did Bob Dylan. So did Miles Davis. So did all the artists worth coming back to, just to see what the crazy bastards are up to now.

Well, I won't have to worry about any of that any more.
Nor why it should even bother me in the first place. All
I know at this point, still staring at the text from a good
friend bringing me the news of Lou Reed's death, is that
when I read it – about an hour ago – I felt not at all like I
did when I heard of the death of Amy Winehouse or John
Peel or Michael Jackson, that it was a sad day for music
and all that blah. I felt instead the way I did when I heard
of the deaths of William S. Burroughs, of Charles Bukowksi,
or indeed Andy Warhol. A deep sense of loss, not of the
music, or the art – we will always have that – but of the
man, whom I saw play live dozens of times over the decades
but whom I only met briefly a handful of times. A complete
one off, utterly misunderstood in his lifetime, poorly treated
and ignorantly undervalued.

In his lifetime he was called, variously, the Godfather
of Punk, the High Priest of Glam, and all sorts of similarly
tremble-tremble sobriquets. The truth is, Lou Reed began
where rock left off. Before him, it was about entertainment.
After him, rock was literary, dark, disturbing, above all,
disquietingly honest. His work belongs not in the same safe
place as The Beatles and the Stones, but next to William S.
Burroughs, Hubert Selby Jr, Andy Warhol and Reed's personal
mentor, the defiled but brilliant Delmore Schwartz. This is
my sincere speed-written, blood-spattered tribute, just the
way Lou, who recorded the first Velvet Underground album
in just four days, would have understood it.

1
ECT

A Jew. A fag. A junkie.

Lou Reed had already achieved the first two of those goals by the time he was 17 and his parents sent him for electroconvulsive therapy, the big new thing in late-1950s America for straightening out its delinquent kids. The experience of which would, not long after, help send him hurtling towards the third.

It wasn't that he was a particularly bad kid, they shrugged. There was just something, well, *wrong* about the boy. The same thing, perhaps, that would later rile so many of his – endless – critics. As if he took an almost perverse delight in defying their buttoned-up expectations, wilfully upsetting whatever applecart their uptight world of Brylcreemed-hair and summer dresses foolishly placed next to him. 'I didn't want to grow up like my old man,' he complained. Well, obviously. Who did? But that doesn't explain why he grew up like Lou Reed.

As a mature artist he would look at his vast back-catalogue and see it as his own version of The Great American Novel, each album its own bloodied chapter. Sure enough, over the course of his zigzagging career, Reed would offer up clues to his real story in many of his songs. Some as straight statements of fact – 'My Old Man', from the wince-inducingly autobiographical *Growing Up In Public*; some more obtusely, yet no less poignantly – 'Smalltown', from *Songs For Drella*, his and John Cale's elegy for their former mentor, Andy Warhol. Yet the line between fact and fiction would always remain hazy. Just as biographical fact merges into character fiction in songs like 'Perfect Day', from his best-known solo album, *Transformer*, so the opposite is true, too, on 'Walk On The Wild Side', from the same album, where whatever fiction there is is confined solely to those coloured girls going doo-dah-doo.

'I'm not in this game for the money or to be a star,' he insisted early on. Of course, they all say that, early on, when they're striving so hard for money and stardom. Lou Reed, who would put you on like an old dress then discard you, crumpled on the floor, actually meant it. It was, perhaps, the most truthfully shocking thing about him.

Lewis Allan Reed was born in Beth El Hospital, Brooklyn, New York, on 2 March 1942. A Pisces, if you're into astrology, so you'll know Lou was a mystic, a psychic, blessed with creative energy and an artistic imagination. You'll also know that, on the flipside, he could be lazy, oversensitive and self-pitying. On the other hand, if you'd ever met Lou, you'd know not to patronise him with such simple-minded 'facts'. Piscean or not, his story was uniquely his, even if he didn't always like owning up to it.

'I don't have a personality of my own,' he once said. A school friend later told Victor Bockris, the Boswell of the

New York scene of Warhol and Burroughs, of Lou Reed and the Velvet Underground, that the teenage Reed suffered from 'shpilkes' – a Yiddisher expression for abrupt nervous energy. 'He can't leave any situation alone or any scab unpicked.'

The Reeds were a well-to-do Jewish family; father Sidney Joseph was a high-flying tax accountant, mother Toby (née Futterman) a former beauty queen. Lewis was the eldest children of three, with a younger sister, Elizabeth, whom he was close to, and a younger brother, whose name, amazingly, appears to have been lost in time – or more likely written out of history by his older brother. When, years later, Reed took to introducing the Velvet Underground's guitarist Doug Yule to audiences as 'my little brother', no one was sure if it was a put-down or a put on. Few thought it might be sincere. (Yule later took over as the Reed-lite front man in the band after Lou quit.)

Growing up comfortable, the fawned-over elder son of an indulgent Jewish mother and a successful businessman father, as Reed told the late feminist writer Caroline Coon, in 1976, 'I know what it's like to have money. So what? My parents were self-made millionaires. On paper they were very rich. They would love me to take over the companies.'

Fat chance. The Reeds were comfortably off but hardly millionaires. His father went to work every morning, something that did not appeal at all to his precious son, who much preferred the doting attentions of his stereotypical Jewish mother. Moving out to the pretty Long Island town of Freeport in 1953, he grew up playing high-school baseball and taking classical piano lessons. Although he later complained about his musical education ('I took classical

music for fifteen fucking years – does that make me legitimate?') it left him with an impressive grasp of musical theory
and composition and 'a natural affinity for music'.

But what he could play and what he actually liked to
listen to on the radio were two different things. He was 15
when Elvis hit No. 1 with 'Heartbreak Hotel', and like the
rest of America first came alive to this new-fangled thing
called rock'n'roll. His tastes soon narrowed down, though,
to a deeper appreciation of more authentically daring artists
like Fats Domino, whose 'Fat Man' he adored, and Little
Richard and the incoherent bliss of 'Tutti Frutti'. Wherever
Little Richard was at, he decided, 'was where I wanted to be'.
He was also into groups closer to home like the Bronx-born
Dion and the Belmonts, whose 1959 hit 'Teenager In Love'
combined the best of rock'n'roll and the lush doo-wop sounds
Lewis was now equally smitten by. Important, too, were vocal
groups like The Five Keys (whose No. 1 version of 'The Glory
Of Love' would find parallel-dimension echoes in Reed's own
later work); The Mystics (whose 1959 hit 'Hushabye' was
co-written by Doc Pomus, who would become an influential
figure in Reed's early career, and in part dedication to whom
he would, decades later, compose an album, *Magic & Loss*);
The Excellents (whose 1962 hit 'Coney Island Baby' would
later provide inspiration for another well-known Reed song
and album); and, surely no coincidence either, The Velvets,
whose 1961 doo-wop hit 'Tonight' was another cherished
addition to his record collection.

Listening to the radio became like a gateway to another
world. An experience Reed would later turn into one of his
most famous Velvet Underground songs, 'Rock And Roll'.

Pestering his parents to buy him a guitar, unlike most budding rock guitarists Reed didn't start at the bottom of the instrument food chain with a cheap imitation, but with an expensive Gretsch Country Gentleman – a green Gretsch 6120, the hollow-bodied electric guitar with signature f-holes that had just appeared on the market, with an endorsement by Chet Akins. It would soon be picked up and made flash by Eddie Cochran and Duane Eddy, both Reed favourites in the mid-1950s.

Of course, his father only agreed to the purchase if his son also took guitar lessons, to complement his classical-piano lessons. But that was precisely the opposite of what the teenager wanted, telling his teacher at their first lesson: 'No, no, no. Teach me how to play the chords for this record.'

Speaking in 2003 to Ian Fortnam, one of the few English writers he got on well with, Reed recalled: 'I studied classical piano and the minute I could play something I started writing new things and I switched to guitar and did the same thing. And the nice thing about rock is, besides the fact that I was in love with it, anyone can play that, and to this day anyone can play a Lou Reed song. Anybody. It's the same essential chords, just various ways of looking at them.'

Armed with 'those three chords' that you could 'play everything on the radio with', he began jamming with a succession of short-lived high-school outfits, teenagers looking for kicks. A chance meeting with a local DJ, Allen Fredericks, whose evening show, *The Night Train*, was a big school favourite, led to a tip-off about how to get a record released. As a result, Lou formed his first semi-professional doo-wop trio, The Shades, quickly renamed The Jades when it was discovered there was already a similar group operating out of New York with the same moniker.

Working as the guitarist and principal songwriter, Reed released a single with The Jades in 1957: a rockabilly/doo-wop hybrid, 'So Blue', credited to Lewis Reed and the band's lead singer, Paul Harris, and on the flipside the Paul Anka-ish 'Leave Her For Me'. A picture taken of The Jades on stage the same year shows a be-quiffed 15-year-old Reed sporting sunglasses, his Gretsch tucked under his arm. Essentially the same look – minus the smart suit jacket and Western-style bowtie – Reed would adopt for the next 30 years.

As a boy, Lou had been chubby, nerdy-looking, nothing special, his curly hair and buck teeth belying the sharply intelligent mind that was starting to emerge. In his teens, anointed by rock'n'roll and newly obsessed with the onscreen heroics of anti-authority figures like James Dean, Marlon Brando and Montgomery Clift, he began to try straightening his hair, and losing weight by simply refusing to eat.

Although their single failed to make any impact commercially, even after it was picked up and re-released on the larger, Paramount-owned Dot Records label, The Jades provided the teenage Lou Reed with his first hard experience of actually performing at gigs, playing shopping malls and what Reed later characterised, in a typically self-mythologising way, in 'some really bad violent places'. Though it seems that the most undignified moments were occasioned by Harris's being so short he would stand on a box to sing harmonies with the group's other vocalist, an extravagantly tall boy with 'a giant mound of snot hanging out of his nose'.

'When I was in high school,' Lou later recalled, 'we had a band and it was originally called The Shades, and somebody knew somebody who knew this guy Bob Shad. Bob Shad worked with Mercury Records and he formed his own little label called Time Records and so we recorded The Shades. Me and these two other guys, I wrote the songs and sang in the background. I wasn't up front. At the same time there was a group from East Meadow, Long Island, called The Bellnotes and they recorded a song called "I've Had It". "I've Had It" became a regional hit. My songs: nothing, zero. So then [the legendary American DJ and self-styled "fifth Beatle"] Murray The K was supposed to play our song one night, but he was sick and his replacement did. I actually heard my song on the radio when I was fourteen, my own song, once. That was it. And I received a royalty check for $2 and 49 cents, as I was fourteen, and that was that. And then Time Records came out with this quartet minus one, you know those kinds of records where it is a band minus one and the minus one is you? It's minus this or minus that and he did that, and somehow he got his hands on Janis Joplin for some little tiny offshoot – and the name The Shades was taken so we had to become The Jades. The record's out on a bootleg somewhere, naturally. But what was really interesting was that the session was run by a guy called Leroy Kirklan, who was the arranger for the Alan Freed Orchestra, of all things. And I got friendly with Leroy. At the session was King Curtis playing sax, can you imagine? I'm fourteen, I've got King Curtis playing on the record. King Curtis. I didn't realise it at the time, but anyway, so I would go up to Harlem to Leroy's apartment with these songs I'd written, trying to see if he could get some doo-wop group or r'n'b group to record some of my songs. So that's the story of The Shades. That's all true.'

The Jades lasted barely a year before Reed lost interest and simply stopped turning up for rehearsals. By then, however, his teenage rebel credentials were firmly established, not least in the eyes of his parents – specifically, the domineering Sidney – and plans were afoot to 'cure' him of his 'ills' before things could get any further out of hand. The eldest, gifted child who had worshipped his father as a little boy, now, as a teenager, refused to hide his disdain for what he saw as his father's boringly bourgeois life. He had also begun to recognise his own – for the 1950s – peculiar, still actually illegal sexuality.

Years later, he would claim he first became aware of his attraction to other boys when he was just 12. Yet there was nowhere in Freeport in the 1950s where he would be able to express his true feelings. Thwarted, frustrated, resentful, instead he would taunt his father by effecting an effeminate way of walking and talking, expecting his indulgent mother to defend him at all costs, whispering to his sister, one girl to another, determined to be the centre of attention, even if it meant screaming the whole house down until he got his way. As he later put it: 'If the forbidden thing is love, then you spend most of your time playing with hate.'

By 1959, Sidney could stand it no longer and made arrangements to have his terrified but still defiant son admitted to Creedmore State Psychiatric Hospital, a state-run facility housing more than 6000 patients. For the next eight weeks, young Lewis underwent hour-long bouts of ECT, three times a week, ostensibly to cure him of his burgeoning homosexuality and, more generally, to purge him of all his other wicked ways. Not least his obsession with both rock'n'roll and anti-authority figures such as James Dean and Marlon Brando. It was a devastating experience that would stay with him, mentally and physically, for the rest of his life.

The adult Reed would recall with disgust 'the thing down your throat so you don't swallow your tongue'. The electrodes methodically attached to his head, held in a brace. His juddering body strapped tight to the bed. At the end of this ordeal, he emerged with his sexuality still intact, but his memory completely wiped, his hands trembling so badly they would never quite recover. Unable to read for several weeks – 'You get to page seventeen and have to go right back to page one again' – he couldn't even sign his own name with a pen; a condition that persisted for the rest of his life, so that years later, after he became famous, fans would complain bitterly that no two Lou Reed autographs ever looked the same. It was so bad lawyers would pore anxiously over the multiple signatures required for his record contracts, each one different to that on the preceding page.

He was eventually put on a tranquilliser, Placidyl, and would continue to take a daily dose for several years. Known on the street as 'jelly bellies', it became a contributory factor in the deadpan expression Reed was to assume, when he could control it, for the rest of his life. He also began having weekly sessions with a psychiatrist. Writers looking back at his life would always cite the 1974 song Reed wrote about his experiences in hospital, 'Kill Your Sons', and its lines about 'two-bit psychiatrists' and the blank families that killed their sons 'until they run, run, run, run, run, run, run, run away'. In truth, though, it could be argued Reed never stopped writing about the therapy that nearly robbed him of his mind. That he would never forgive the ice-cold father who put him in the ward or the bloodless doctors who performed the 'therapy' upon him. That he would never trust anyone again until his life was almost over, throwing up a shield that only the similarly damaged could ever truly see through. And then, only for short periods, while Lou let 'em, a personal favour he would sooner or later withdraw with sometimes immense ferocity.

Run away he did. Though not, as might be imagined, straight from the plush family home in Long Island into a roach-infested loft in New York's Greenwich Village, but by enrolling, in 1961, at Syracuse University, in upstate New York, where he studied for – and eventually got – a BA in English. A top-drawer American campus, Syracuse was a nineteenth-century intellectual hotbed noted for having produced several prominent American politicians, business leaders, scientists and athletes. It was also home to several branches of the arts, and the alma mater of TV and film stars like Peter Falk (best known now for *Columbo*), the award-winning stage actor and director Frank Langella (best known now for *Frost/Nixon*) and that archetypal New Yorker, the character actor Jerry Stiller (*Seinfeld*, *King Of Queens*, et al).

More significantly, Syracuse was also now the home of the American poet and short-story writer Delmore Schwartz. Then teaching a creative writing class, Schwartz became a father figure to the 19-year-old Reed, who was thrilled to be in the presence of a genuine American icon, albeit one already on the slide, personally and professionally. Having become the youngest-ever recipient of the Bollingen Prize the year before, for his collection *Summer Knowledge: New and Selected Poems*, Schwartz appeared to be at his artistic peak. Born, like Reed, in Brooklyn, in 1913, Schwartz was another hypersensitive child whose Romanian Jewish immigrant parents had left him feeling isolated and resentful in a world that just didn't care. He claimed their divorce when he was nine had had a profound effect upon him. But those who knew him suspected it was the sudden death of his wealthy father, in 1930, that really changed him. Inheriting just a fraction of the fortune he expected, Schwartz remained resentful for the rest of his life.

Nevertheless, his academic career was distinguished enough to find him studying as a graduate in philosophy at Harvard University, where he was mentored by the English mathematician and philosopher Alfred North Whitehead – before dropping out, on the eve of publication, in the first issue of the *Partisan Review*, in 1937, of his infamous short story, 'In Dreams Begin Responsibilities', a thinly veiled account of his parents' failed marriage.

When this and other works were then published as his first book, also titled *In Dreams Begin Responsibilities*, the following year, his reputation seemed made. He was 25, the talk of the town in New York, where he began receiving praise from the likes of Ezra Pound, T. S. Eliot and William Carlos Williams. Over the next 20 years, Schwartz published a string of well-received poems, stories and plays; his major themes the immeasurable distance between the voice inside one's head and the catastrophically disconnected world outside it. He also enjoyed spells as editor of the *Partisan Review* and, later, the *New Republic*.

Things began to turn sour in 1943, when his six-year marriage to Gertrude Buckman, another contributor to the *Partisan Review*, ended in divorce. Even harder for him to take, however, was the unexpectedly hostile response that same year to his epic poem, *Genesis*, which he had dreamed would be seen as a masterpiece worthy to stand alongside similarly Modernist landmarks such as Eliot's *The Waste Land* and Pound's *The Cantos*. He continued to rampage across the American literary landscape, becoming close friends with the poet Robert Lowell, whom he shared a house with in Cambridge, Massachusetts, in 1946 – a time Lowell recalled in his 1959 poem 'To Delmore Schwartz', describing them as 'underseas fellows, nobly mad / we talked away our friends'. But when a second marriage, this time to the much younger novelist, Elizabeth Pollet, ended soon after in another divorce, it was the start of a steep downward spiral that would result, by the time he began teaching at Syracuse 15 years later, in Schwartz retreating into alcohol and amphetamines, and the increasingly hysterical, if still brilliant, sound of his own voice above all others.

By the time Reed began attending his creative-writing classes, in 1961, Schwartz was still considered a great conversationalist and art scene bon viveur – a familiar face at the famous White Horse Tavern in Greenwich Village, where the regular clientele of artists, writers and their eager followers still found time for his ever more outlandish behaviour. And the damaged, mixed-up boy from Long Island fell instantly under his spell. When he discovered that, like him, Schwartz had undergone electro-convulsive therapy at one point, to try and cure him of his own manic depression, Lou felt sure he'd found a kindred spirit.

As Reed later recalled in a 1973 interview with fellow New York writer-artist Bruce Pollock: 'Delmore Schwartz was the unhappiest man I ever met in my life and the smartest... till I met Andy Warhol. He didn't use curse words till age thirty. His mother wouldn't allow him. His worst fears were realised when he died and they put him in a plot next to her. Once, drunk in a Syracuse bar, he said, "If you sell out, Lou, I'm gonna get ya." I hadn't thought about doing anything let alone selling out. Two years later, he was gone.' Lou added: 'I'm just delighted I got to know him. It would have been tragic not to have met him. Things have occurred where Delmore's words float right across. Very few people do it to ya. He was one.'

It wasn't long before the relationship had progressed far beyond the usual bounds of teacher–student. They would stay up all night, crazed on speed, then begin drinking at eight the following morning. 'He'd order five drinks at once,' remembered Lou. 'He was also one of the funniest people I ever met in my life.' It was in Schwartz's class that Reed discovered as well contemporary works by William S. Burroughs, Jack Kerouac, Raymond Chandler and the writer he would most resemble in his own early work, the Brooklyn-born junkie Hubert Selby Jr, whose work throughout the 1960s would suffer the same level of critical opprobrium and gross misunderstanding among the literati as the Velvet Underground would endure in their even more narrow artistic sphere.

There was another unexpected offshoot of attending Schwartz's classes at Syracuse, however, that would rekindle his interest in the electric guitar: meeting another suburban middle-class escapee from Long Island, named Sterling Morrison. Living in the same dorm, Sterling introduced himself after overhearing Lou playing loud electric guitar in his room. Lou turned his new friend on to Delmore. Sterling thought it might be better just to stick to their guitars. As Morrison told the Canadian writer and filmmaker Mary Harron, in 1981: 'Delmore was a brilliant poet, but he had a clinical case of paranoia. He thought he was being persecuted by Nelson Rockefeller, and eventually he decided that Lou and I were both Rockefeller's spies.'

Still harbouring ambitions to make it somehow as a rock'n'roll singer – in 1960, he had persuaded Time to let him record a solo single, still as Lewis Reed, the cringe-inducingly jolly 'Merry Go Round' and the more pleasingly raunchy 'Your Love' – the latter sung in the sort of full-bore vibrato-rattling voice he would seem incapable of for the rest of his career. Neither track was eventually released (at least, not until years later after he'd become a star) and by the time he got to Syracuse Lou had shelved his ambitions to be a pop star in favour of his studies of modern American literature, and a new part-time role as a DJ on the college radio station, mixing his beloved doo-wop 45s with out-there experimental recordings by Pierre Boulez, Ornette Coleman and the early folk-protest of Bob Dylan.

At the prompting of Sterling Morrison, though, he now began hanging out with other aspiring Syracuse rock musos like Felix Cavaliere (later of The Young Rascals), Mike Esposito (of The Blues Magoos) and another Brooklyn-born singer-songwriter, named Garland Jeffreys. This resulted in a cluster of here-today-gone-later-today student groups of varying degrees of seriousness like Moses and His Brothers, Pasha and the Prophets, LA and the El Dorados, and other dumb names that made them laugh. Yet it was this heady juxtaposition of wild Beat Lit and comparatively innocent dance-rock, he later claimed, that led him to writing such early classics as 'Heroin' – inspired by Selby Jr's harrowing debut novel *Last Exit To Brooklyn* – and 'Venus In Furs' – title taken from the 1869 novel by Leopold von Sacher-Masoch that detailed the author's real-life S&M fantasies; impossibly proposed music that would stretch pop and rock to its 1960s outer limits. A lot of these early lyrics began as short stories and poems, in emulation of his hero Delmore. He even sent a few examples of his work to the *New Yorker*, who didn't like what they saw at all and roundly rejected them. So he sent stuff instead to smaller, more niche poetry publications like the *Kenyon Review* and the *Paris Review* – but again all he got in return were rejection letters, when they could be bothered to respond at all.

It was also at college, he later fessed up, that he had his first openly gay love affair. He was having a fairly serious affair with a female Syracuse student at the time, named Shelley Albin, and claimed the momentary gay flirtation was 'never consummated'. But it was a first important step towards the kind of self-actualisation he knew he would never have been able to achieve if he'd stayed home in Freeport. He also formed a taste for drugs; not merely the 'purple hearts' Delmore used to stay crazy, nor just the pot that was now becoming the norm on college campuses all over America, but seriously Burroughsian elixirs like heroin, which he later claimed to have been introduced to by a 'mashed-in-faced Negro' local drug dealer. Along with his first fix, said Reed, the dealer also gave him hepatitis – 'bad blood' – a particularly chilling confession, if true, given his struggle in later life with liver disease.

Nevertheless, these were formative experiences; things that, like the nightmare of his ECT experience, he saw as feeding the creative fires; creating songs and stories and poems just waiting to be written. By the time he graduated with his BA in English in 1964, Lou Reed, as everybody now knew him bar his parents (whom he'd vowed he'd never see again, yet returned to live with, off and on, until 1965), was ready to take on the world. That's what he told himself anyway.

He had originally thought he might stay on at Syracuse for another year doing post-grad courses in journalism and drama. But he grew too impatient for one – disgusted after being chastised for 'interject[ing]' his own opinion into a report he'd written: 'I quit!' – and too self-aware for the other – 'I couldn't cut the mustard [as an actor] but I was a good director.' Out of college and out of work, he found himself being drafted for the US army; then engaged in a rapidly escalating war in Vietnam. But he was rejected on the grounds that he was 'mentally unfit – crazy'. Shorthand, no doubt, for the fact that his record showed a college graduate with a background in mental illness and a sexual orientation still considered illegal and, moreover, specifically forbidden in the US Armed Forces.

Finally, in October 1964, he found something he could hold on to when he was offered a job at the offices of Pickwick Records. A lucky break he tended to shrug off in later life. 'I met somebody who said, "You write songs. So and so could use a songwriter. A staff-songwriter. Would you be interested?" So I said yeah.' That somebody was Pickwick's in-house producer,

Terry Phillips, and though neither of them knew it, this would be the unlikely start of Reed's career as a singer-songwriter. In those long ago, pre-internet days when radio was the only gatekeeper between a hit and a miss, companies like Pickwick thrived on creating cheaply made, copycat hits that would be sold, principally, as budget-priced discs in supermarkets and chain stores. Reed's job was to write and record albums – long players – that would claim to be the work of a handful of different new groups, yet were all made by the same team of in-house hacks, led by Lou, and sold for 99 cents.

At first it was fun churning out such gems as 'Johnny Can't Surf No More', 'Let The Wedding Bells Ring' and a hotrod song, released under the nom de plume of The Beachnuts, a proto-Velvet Underground low-slung rocker with Lou on vocals and guitar – *being paid to manufacture musical dross, how fabulous!* But the novelty of writing songs-by-numbers soon wore off, making him yearn for the more unbidden, uninhibited, frankly artier realms of experimental music. Or music, at least, that didn't taste just of lollipops. Even the arrival for the first time into the American charts of The Beatles – who managed to chalk up no fewer than four No. 1 LPs in 1964 – failed to ignite his interest. As he so memorably put it, years later: 'The Beatles were innocent of the world.' Adding in the same breath: 'I, after all, had had jaundice.'

Speaking in 2003, however, Reed recalled his time at Pickwick as 'great experience. It was just me and these three other guys writing essentially what would be called hack stuff, and a lot of that stuff has found its way onto bootlegs amazingly enough. "Psycle Annie" is an example of that kind of thing. But there was one that I really liked that I wrote with one of those guys called "Love Can Make You Cry" and I've never been able to find a copy of that. That actually was a good song. "Psycle Annie", that was one of those hotrod songs, and I wrote another one: "Let The Wedding Bells Ring". Have you heard that track? Well, the guy's got a car in high school, she wants to get married, he doesn't have enough money so he enters a race and gets killed. So, you know, they came in the room and said write us twenty rock'n'roll death songs... You know, "Tell Laura I Love Her", those kinds of things. So we did, and it was a great experience because you got to record them... The writing is nothing, but it's like training. I've only had two or three real jobs in my life. None of them lasted very long, but one of them was to file the burr off a nut in a factory, and that's what this was.'

Finally, his frustration grew too much and he decided to make his day go a little easier by presenting Phillips with a musical wolf in sheep's clothing: a horribly cynical, bitingly funny – if you got the joke – new dance-craze tune called 'The Ostrich'. The suits at Pickwick didn't catch on – probably barely listened – just gave their youngest, brightest boy his head and told him they would release it locally and, if the dance actually caught on, begin trying to push it nationally. But what Lou sold to them as the next in a then trendy line in dance-craze records, from Chubby Checker's 'The Twist' and 'It's Pony Time' to Dee Dee Sharp's 'Do The Bird', was more than just the usual Pickwick me-too knock-off. Brazenly lifting the bass riff from the Crystals' 1963 chart hit from the previous year, 'Then He Kissed Me', a furiously bored Reed tuned all the strings on his guitar to the same note.

'I did that because I saw this guy called Jerry Vance do that. Jerry Vance was not an advanced avant-garde guy. He was just screwing around. And he didn't realise what he had, but I did.' Adding dance-step lyrics that deliberately parodied the style of such records – crowing: 'Take a step forward… Step on your face!' – and instead of a chorus added some nerve-jangling screaming. Intended to be both catchy enough to fool the dullards, as he saw it, that actually bought such records, yet just creepy enough to get him sniggering into his lit joint as he rattled away on his one-note guitar, what he had inadvertently achieved was almost a template for the sound he would later explore in such alarming depth in groundbreaking Velvet Underground songs like 'Sister Ray'. Even the boot-stomping rhythm, veering out of control as it collides into a monstrous face-pounding climax, could be seen as the proto-Velvets sound, as evinced on future classics like 'I'm Waiting For The Man' and 'White Light/White Heat'.

Despite its abject failure as a single to either elicit radio play or sell in anything even approaching double figures – indeed, its complete lack of regard among anybody at the time outside Lou's own friends whenever they got high – Reed seemed to acknowledge the door he had opened with 'The Ostrich'; to the point where on the debut Velvet Underground album, released two years later, he credited himself as playing 'Ostrich Guitar'. Nearly 50 years later, in some of his final interviews, Lou Reed was still talking up his unpatented one-note 'ostrich tuning'. It wasn't just the music it symbolised in his mind, though; it was what the choice to make that record stood for, to him personally. Working for a company that existed solely for commercial reasons, there was no gain to be made in trying to subvert that cause, not like there would be when recording as a legitimate solo artist for a major record label. He just couldn't help himself. A contrarian from his curly-haired head to his pointy-boot toes, from here on in Lou Reed would forge a career out of always doing what was least expected – often what was least wanted – of him. As an artist, as a person, as a guy alone in the world, the living embodiment of Marlon Brando's fictional anti-hero who, when asked what he's rebelling against, answers simply: 'Whatta ya got?'

Unlike the onscreen Brando, though, the onstage Reed was impossible to second-guess. This was the rebel who would rather poke out his own eyes than have to sit around listening to other so-called rebels; an imposter in both worlds, who could never be pinned down for long: not even by himself.

No one can make it entirely on their own, though, and it was now that Reed met the person who would most aid him in his next step: a Royal College of Music drop-out recently arrived from London named John Cale. Born a week short of Lou's birthday, John Cale would become the musically intellectual twin to Reed's instinctively provocative phrase-maker: the European classicist whose influence would help refine the American rock'n'roller, so that together they might create a form of music that overlapped into something distinctively its own; something new and possibly even dangerous.

Again, it was 'The Ostrich' which inadvertently made it happen. When somehow, against the odds, Terry Phillips secured a spot for the record to be performed on *American Bandstand* – then the longest-running Variety show on American TV, fronted by another former Syracuse alumnus, Dick Clark – he hastily put together a fictitious band for the occasion, which included Cale, an accomplished viola player with a side-interest in bass, whom he had recently met and assumed must be a pop musician on the basis that he had long hair. Lou would front the group – which he named, tongue still determinedly in cheek, The Primitives – with two other friends of Cale's, the sculptor Walter de Maria on drums and fellow musical student Tony Conrad on keyboards.

According to Cale, in his 1999 autobiography, *What's Welsh For Zen*, they saw it as a 'lark', getting on TV and playing a couple of shows. No biggie. The experience, reflected Cale, although limited, offered the two new friends 'the opportunity to connect.'

Both men found something in the other that completed them, musically and culturally. Having abandoned the staid environs of London's Royal College, Cale had already performed with John Cage, where his knowledge of Stockhausen had quickly escalated into performances in which the climax involved taking an axe to his piano. Having studied composition with Aaron Copland he arrived in New York early in 1965 on a Leonard Bernstein scholarship. Almost immediately he found himself invited to play electric viola in La Monte Young's Theater of Eternal Music, a musical arena where then radical new ideas about minimalism – in particular the use of lengthy, sustained tones played at maximum volume – seemed weirdly to echo his new friend Lou's own little 'experiment' with the guitar on 'The Ostrich'.

Reed also offered the young Welshman the opportunity to more fully immerse himself in the sheer hustle of downtown New York, whose cheap, roach-infested 'studio' apartments – small, single, furniture-less rooms – intermingled with the uptown flow of art galleries, musical theatre and the warped bohemia of Times Square where tourists were warned not to go yet held an inexorable pull for new-in-town 22-year-old thrill-seekers like Reed and Cale.

What Lou saw in John was instant access to the kind of European avant-gardism not even Delmore Schwartz had been able to summon for him. John was not easily impressed and when Lou pulled out an acoustic guitar and played him two new songs he'd written, called 'Heroin' and 'Waiting For The Man', Cale dismissed them as the sub-Dylan ramblings of a would-be folkie. Lou was aghast, embarrassed, limp. Then something snagged John's attention and he asked to look at the lyrics that Lou had typed up so neatly. Recognising 'a tremendous literary quality in his songs', though he wasn't an aficionado of rock'n'roll music the way Lou clearly was, he realised 'He was writing about things other people weren't.'

In the cold spring of 1965, Lou Reed quit his job at Pickwick, after it became clear that Terry Phillips was not interested in allowing him to record any more of his original songs. Instead he began hanging out at John Cale's tiny apartment at 56 Ludlow Street, on the low-rent Lower East Side, where it was often so cold they would sit around in sweaters and coats, banging their boots on the floor for warmth. It helped if they played their instruments, so they began rehearsing, though for what exactly no one was yet entirely sure, just that it wouldn't be like what else was going on then in midtown Manhattan, whose regular club acts still wore tight suits and skinny ties. Lou could do his own songs and John would somehow make them fit into what he was really interested in too, which was more to do with jazz and classical music, though really not even that. Sterling Morrison was drafted in to fill out the line-up and another of John's friends from Young's Eternal Music collective, named Angus MacLise, who had also spent years studying eastern musical percussion in Greece and India, became their drummer.

At first they were going to keep the name The Primitives. Then they changed their minds and went for The Warlocks. Then it was The Falling Spikes – a short-lived folk trio comprising Reed, Cale and Elektrah Lobel, which got as far as performing at the Village's most famous club haunt, Café Wha?. But the jokes grew thinner as the music grew more unfriendly and weathered, and when they found an old paperback of *Venus In Furs* lying around (left by Tony Conrad, whom Cale had taken over the apartment from) the coincidence seemed too much for Lou, who suggested they make it the name of their new group. No one said yes, but no one said no.

A non-committal shrug sealed the deal.

2
Flowers Of Evil

Some say the 1960s actually began late, not really getting off the ground until Friday, 5 October 1962: the day the first James Bond movie, *Dr No*, premiered in London, and, coincidentally, the day The Beatles released their first single, 'Love Me Do'.

One might equally argue that the 1970s arrived indecently early, on 12 March 1967: the day of the release of the album *The Velvet Underground & Nico*. It did not cause anything like the same seismic cultural earthquake as either The Beatles or James Bond, of course. Indeed, it barely registered on the radar of more than a handful of New York scenesters who were far too cool to make a big deal of it anyway. Their record company, Verve, rightfully considered it a dreadful flop. The critics wrinkled their noses and wrote it off as an unfortunate aberration. Had it not also come with the Andy Warhol imprimatur, frankly no one would probably have given a shit.

'Our favourite quote,' Lou said of the criticism the Velvet Underground faced, was: 'the flowers of evil are in bloom. Someone has to stamp them out before they spread.'

As the years crept by, though, and successive generations of music journalists, rock musicians, filmmakers, novelists, biographers, art historians and those that were merely drug-curious or sex-craven made their way back to it, metaphorically unpeeling the banana that served as its daintily obscene cover image, finding themselves not-so-innocent bystanders to a cultural phenomenon that continues to seep through the musical and social landscape of the twenty-first century like poisoned blood through a yellowed bandage.

Musicologists and pop historians are fond of likening the release the same year of The Beatles' *Sgt Pepper's Lonely Hearts Club Band* album as the moment the world turned, like the newest TVs then on the market, from black-and-white into colour. It's a sweet pop image. But if true, then it is *The Velvet Underground & Nico* that would eventually lead pop and its older brother rock away from its brightly coloured love-is-all-you-need paradise and down towards that dark room at the end of the dimly-lit corridor where all our deepest fears and insecurities, our worst lusts and most criminal desires reside, breathing in cigarette smoke and stinking of cold sweat; shameful and unrepentant, elitist and aloof; worldly and unfriendly. Unlike The Beatles, who were all come-on-in-the-water's-fine, and were universally loved and forgiven anything for it, the Velvet Underground were get-out-I-hate-you, and were loved only after they were gone, rotted, ploughed into the earth and – almost – forgotten. Even by Andy Warhol who never forgot a thing. Right, Lou?

The funny thing is, it wasn't meant to be this way. Reed and Cale – and Morrison and MacLise – knew they were onto something as they kept going at the Ludlow Street loft, into the summer of 1965. But they thought it was something they would be able to share, be applauded for even, by their contemporaries, never guessing that what they were doing was so far away from what was already considered the rock norm – even as sales of LPs were beginning to overtake those of singles for the first time, and artists like Frank Zappa, Love and The Doors were beginning to stake their own claims for the outer fringes of what rock could do, where it might go – that they would be considered a sick joke, one of Andy's passing fancies, before they would ever be considered musicians who might actually have something to say.

The first hint of the unthinking disdain that lay ahead came when Cale, on a brief visit back to London, in July 1965, tried to slip a copy of their demo tape to Marianne Faithfull in the hope that she might play it for Mick Jagger and that, suitably wowed, the Rolling Stones singer would return with an offer of immediate help. Money, studio time, recognition, whatever. But Faithfull was too wrapped up in her own problems to pay attention and Jagger too used to approaches from other money-for-nothing musicians. (Years later, the same five-song tape would turn up on the 1995 Velvets box set, *Peel Slowly And See*, and one can only be thankful, in retrospect, that Jagger never bothered to play the tape, consisting as it does of truly dreadful versions of songs that, in radically revamped form, would soon enter the rock pantheon, including an ethereal version of 'Venus In Furs' sung by Cale; an acoustic 'Heroin', sung by Reed with a terrible Dylan yaw to his phrasing; a bizarrely country-tinged 'I'm Waiting For The Man', which sounds like Hank Williams on downers, interspersed with Cale reciting sections in 'posh' English; and 'All Tomorrow's Parties', even more unnervingly Dylan-esque with its folksy acoustic guitar and baleful harmony vocals. Worse still were the additional two tracks that didn't make it to the first Velvets album: 'Wrap Your Troubles In Dreams', a mordant Falling Spikes folk leftover; and most hair-raising the acoustic-and-harmonica sub-Dylan ditty 'Prominent Man', prompting the question: just how much Placidyl had Lou had that day?) What Cale did return from London with, though, was a pile of singles from new high-energy English acts like The Who, The Kinks and the Small Faces. Inspired, he urged Reed to step up his own performances, drop the Dylan twang and go for broke with a sound that relied less on acoustic guitar and more on Cale's ostinato piano and droning repetitive-to-the-point-of-screaming viola.

Angus MacLise also helped confirm their new direction when he talked the underground filmmaker Piero Heliczer – whose film that year, *Dirt*, the director summed up as 'two nuns take a bath, then meet a sailor on the Staten Island Ferry' – into letting them perform for him, when MacLise helped Heliczer stage 'a ritual happening' at the Cinématèque on Great Jones Street. Titled *The Launching Of The Dream Weapon* and comprising a mélange of film, music, dancers, lights and poetry, it became a forerunner of the newly dubbed 'mixed-media' shows that Andy Warhol was about to lay his own claim to.

Performing in an environment that appeared to appreciate their abstract, otherworldly noise as an 'art happening' was a revelation which immediately opened up the nascent band's minds to not just what they played but how they could play and where. As Sterling Morrison later recalled: '... the path suddenly became clear. [We] could work on music that was different from ordinary rock'n'roll since Piero had given [us] a context to perform it in.' Over the next few weeks this early version of the Velvet Underground would appear in similar roles at other screenings at the Cinématèque, including, most fittingly, a night of Kenneth Anger's *Scorpio Rising*, which mixed occult themes alongside biker imagery, Catholicism, Nazism and whatever else the audience's drug-blasted minds could read into it.

None of these gigs paid money, though; until, finally, they were offered $75 by Al Aronowitz to perform at a high school in Summit, New Jersey. Aronowitz was a hip American rock writer then best known for introducing Bob Dylan to The Beatles, and who, by 1965, was hanging out with Brian Jones of the Stones while writing for the *Saturday Evening Post* and managing a group called the Myddle Class. It sounded like another perfect Velvet Underground gig but MacLise refused to take part because he was in it solely for the art, not the money.

Lou, who came from money but never had any of his own, didn't care either way. What he seized on was the chance to get rid of MacLise, whom he had felt threatened by from the start. Angus and John were cut from the same musical cloth, had been to the same schools, knew best about all the things Lou didn't. And while they had been happy enough to have Lou as their mouthpiece, even performing most of his songs, he had never quite felt in control enough of the group. It was always John and Angus and Lou and Sterling. With Angus gone, Lou could start to reassert his influence again. When Sterling suggested drafting in the younger sister of a friend of his, named Maureen Tucker, Cale initially baulked at the idea of having a girl in the group, which only made Lou more determined to make it happen. Morrison, who'd known Tucker since she was 12, was equally staunch on the subject. 'He was like my pain-in-the-ass big brother,' she recalled. Lou got his way. Angus was out – for good.

Nineteen-year-old 'Moe', as she preferred to be known, had been the tub-thumping drummer in an amateur all-girl band. Born in Levittown, New York, in 1946, she'd recently dropped out of Ithaca College and was earning $60 a week working as a keypunch operator for IBM when she got the call from Sterling. She agreed to come and play but she was not about to give up her day job, she decided. 'John, Lou and Sterling were living in terrible places,' she recalled for Phil Sutcliffe, in 1992. 'They used to go out on the street and look for wood to burn in the fireplace. It wasn't romantic, it stank.' You certainly get the sense of Tucker's distance from the others when you look now at those grainy black-and-white pictures of the early Velvets, standing around in their shades and gloomy faces. The only one not posing – or even 'not posing' – is Moe, whose profound lack of interest in what for others would be considered the most exotic of surroundings is probably only matched by the stoic expression Stones drummer Charlie Watts would perfect over the next 50 years. And it made Lou and John feel more secure knowing Moe would never question where they were going with the band. As she would later tell Richard North: 'I did not want to be the most prominent.' As a result, 'Everybody treated me great.' They also 'loved the fact that I didn't take drugs. I think they respected me for that. Nobody ever tried to talk me into taking them; being in a movie or anything I didn't want to do. It was no big deal.'

And yet, seemingly unobtrusive though it was, what Moe's playing – straight to the point, foregoing the use of cymbals, hi-hat and big bass drum, no use even for a drum stool, preferring instead as she did to stand at her work space, relying merely on tom-toms and a metronomic, almost tribal form of percussion for the beat – brought to the Velvet Underground became as much a signature part of their sound as that of Cale's crazed viola, Reed's deadpan voice and Morrison's slack-jawed bass. 'I think Maureen Tucker is a genius drummer,' Lou declared in 2003. 'She's one of the great people. Her style of drumming, that she invented, is amazing, and you still see occasional groups where the guy will be playing standing up. But I'm surprised that the other girl drummers were very obsessed with being like a guy drummer, not with following Maureen's lead, which is standing up, because it adds some strength.'

Impressed by the new line-up's performance in New Jersey, Aronowitz excitedly recommended them to the management of the Café Bizarre on Bleecker Street, in Greenwich Village, where they began a two-week engagement in December 1965. It was not a success. Removed from the comfort zone of the self-consciously artsy crowds they had been playing to at underground film nights, they found out the hard way just how limited their appeal was to an everyday downtown New York crowd looking for a drink and a good time. Cale would later only half-jokingly recall how the only people who stayed for their shows were people too drunk to leave. The band began using their time onstage as glorified improv sessions, elongating numbers and turning up the feedback. When the owners, out of pocket and out of patience, insisted they play an extra-long set on Christmas Eve, the band responded in kind, by launching into a mammoth version of their, so far, most convoluted number, a cacophonous song-poem they called 'The Black Angel's Death Song'; essentially a long rant by Reed, half sung, half hissed, that Cale smothered in a discordant sonic hailstorm of manic electric viola. When it was finally over the owner grabbed Sterling Morrison and told him: 'If you play that song one more time you're fired!' They immediately struck into the song again, only this time at twice the length and teeth-grating power. And were duly fired. The coming New Year of 1966 did not look to be a promising one. John still had his scholarship to eke out a living with, Moe still had her day job, but Lou and Sterling were forced to look for casual work; factory and bar jobs that would barely see them through the holidays.

Fate, however, was about to take another, more meaningful hand in things, when yet another underground filmmaker then making the scene in the Village, named Barbara Rubin, told Andy Warhol he should check out the group. Already approaching the peak of a career begun in commercial art but now encompassing major gallery shows in New York and Los Angeles, Warhol had gone from minor avant-garde artist to mainstream cultural icon in 1962 with his headline-grabbing exhibition of 32 paintings each depicting a subtly different aspect of a Campbell's Soup can. From that time on, Andy Warhol's name became synonymous with a whole new genre – Pop Art – that perfectly reflected the bright, everything-is-new world of the 1960s.

At the time he first espied the Velvet Underground and instantly fell for the skinny legs and haughty expression of their 23-year-old singer, Warhol had lately branched out into film, releasing 14 movies between 1963 and '65 alone – along with more than 80 random 'shorts', depicting various visitors to his studio, from the daringly unknown drag queens of the nearby Bowery to Hollywood stars like Dennis Hopper and Jack Nicholson. Warhol's films, short or long, were unlike anything seen before even in the anything-goes world of the New York underground. His first feature, *Sleep*, in 1963, was a long, five-hour take of his friend and fellow artist John Giorno sleeping. His second, *Kiss*, released the same year, was a 50-minute meditation on couples – man and woman, woman and woman, man and man – kissing for three and a half minutes each. Subsequent titles – often featuring the same, or a similar, revolving cast of characters, many of whom had never previously been before a camera, such as Gerard Malanga (who liked to carry a whip), Edie Sedgwick (the prettiest butterfly, whose wings would soon be pulled off), Brigid Polk (so named because she liked to give people 'a poke' from syringes filled with vitamins and amphetamines), and drag queens straight off the street such as Jackie Curtis and Candy Darling, and the transgender Holly Woodlawn, all of whom would become people Lou wrote songs about (not least 'Walk On The Wild Side', which featured all three of the last-named) – included *Blow Job*, *Taylor Mead's Ass*, *Chelsea Girls* and, most challenging of all, *Empire*: over eight hours of continuous slow-motion footage of the Empire State Building.

Critics were, variously, puzzled, shocked, staunchly unshocked, frankly bored, often appalled, but they couldn't stop writing about them. Meanwhile sales of Warhol's increasingly famous silkscreens – a process akin to print-making that allowed him to reproduce colour images in ever-varying multiples – of American icons, including Elvis Presley, Marilyn Monroe, Elizabeth Taylor and Marlon Brando, and other cultural signifiers, such as dollar bills, electric chairs, Coke bottles and so on, was turning him into the hippest, most famous and, ultimately, most collectible American artist in the world. He produced this tsunami of work at a studio he dubbed 'The Factory', on the fifth floor of an abandoned building on East 47th Street, in midtown Manhattan, where with the help of various acolytes like Billy Name (who would sleep at The Factory in a closet) he lined the floor and walls in silver, and encouraged the 24-hour attention of every larger-than-life character, it seemed, that happened to be passing through, whether they be named Bob Dylan, Jim Morrison, Leonard Cohen or Warhol's own self-made 'superstars' like Ultra Violet (actually a French-American artist named Isabelle Collin Dufresne) and 'Baby' Jane Holzer (née Bruckenfeld; an art collector with a wealthy husband).

By the time his friend Barbara Rubin began talking Andy's ear off about this new group she'd seen, Warhol was beginning to develop an interest in the burgeoning pop scene, and its potential for new 'art', as evinced by the evolution of groups like The Beatles and closer-to-home groups like The Lovin' Spoonful, The Mamas & The Papas and, of course, Bob Dylan. It was Rubin who persuaded Andy – along with Factory staple Gerard Malanga – to accompany her to one of the last Café Bizarre shows. Andy was doing 'movies with real people, what you see is what you get'.

Now he thought how 'fabulous' it would be to make music with 'real' people. Lou Reed was equally smitten with the sallow-skinned, bewigged Warhol.

'I loved him on sight,' Lou smilingly recalled. 'He was obviously one of us. He was right. I didn't know who he was, I wasn't aware of any of that, amazingly enough. But he was obviously a kindred spirit if ever there was one, and so smart with charisma to spare. But really so smart, and for a, quote, "passive" guy, he took over everything. He was the leader, which would be very surprising for a lot of people to work out. He was in charge of us, everyone. You look towards Andy, the least likely person, but in fact the most likely. He was so smart, so talented and twenty-four hours a day, going at it. Plus, he had a vision. He was driven and he had a vision to fulfil. And I fit in like a hand in a glove. Bingo. Interest? The same. Vision? Equivalent. Different world and he just incorporated us. It was amazing. I mean, if you think in retrospect how does something like that happen? It's unbelievable. I went from being with Delmore Schwartz, who taught me so much about writing, and then I'm there with Andy where you get all the rest of it.'

In fact, the first thing Warhol did was try and replace Lou as the singer with an entirely different voice and presence named Nico. The decision stemmed from an observation made by Andy's business manager, Paul Morrissey, who was not only convinced that Lou 'didn't have the personality' to be the front man, but felt, more acutely, that it would be more interesting, as he put it to the biographer Victor Bockris, to have 'something beautiful' on the stage to 'counteract the screeching ugliness they were trying to sell'.

This 'something beautiful' was a German actress and model, Nico. Born in Cologne, in 1938, Christa Päffgen had been 'discovered' as a model when she was 16 by the photographer Herbert Tobias, who nicknamed her 'Nico' after his friend the filmmaker Nikos Papatakis. By 17, she was living in Paris, where she became the favoured face of Coco Chanel. By the time she was 20 she had travelled to New York, learned to speak English, Spanish and French, and landed a small role in Alberto Lattuada's film *La Tempesta*. The same year she also appeared in Rudolph Maté's *For The First Time*. In 1959, visiting Cinecittà studios in Rome, where Federico Fellini was shooting *La Dolce Vita*, enchanted by her ethereal beauty the wily old director built in a small part for her – playing herself.

Arriving at The Factory one day in 1965, on the arm of the doomed Stone, Brian Jones, Andy was equally smitten, though in a quite different way. Nico, taking Lee Strasberg's 'method' acting class, had appeared on the cover of the jazz pianist Bill Evans' 1962 album, *Moon Beams*, and had starred, two years earlier, in Jacques Poitrenaud's *Strip-Tease* – for which she had also sung the soundtrack's title song, written by Serge Gainsbourg, though not eventually released until 2001, when it was included on the compilation *Le Cinéma de Serge*. In 1962, she'd given birth to a son, Christian Aaron 'Ari' Päffgen, whose father was the French screen legend Alain Delon (the child was later adopted and raised by Delon's mother and father, taking their name, Boulogne).

She was exactly the kind of exotic creature that Andy fawned over and begged to film and take pictures of, to know and consume like a bottle of the most expensive rare wine. He immediately pressed Lou to let Nico take over the spotlight onstage with the Velvets, and to write some songs especially for her to sing. Lou was affronted, appalled – how would John Lennon have reacted had Brian Epstein suggested bringing in Cilla Black to front The Beatles early on? – yet street-smart enough not to blow it with the rest of the Factory goons looking on. He tentatively agreed – with one caveat: Nico would not actually join the band, she would still be an artist in her own right: hence, the Velvet Underground *and* Nico. It was a shrewd move and one that both flattered Nico and blindsided Warhol and Morrissey.

Everything was happening so fast, it was, said Lou, 'Very hard to believe. I mean, you know, it's not something that you would want to bet on, or plan on. On the other hand... I was there. I was available. Did anyone notice? No. Did anyone care about us? No. And then who walks in? There you go – opportunity of a lifetime. You know, Andy had a vision, and he had this way of looking at it. "Have a chanteuse", why not? That sounds like fun. What are we hard-core, or something? We were very hard-core about the music and the lyrics and the approach, but the rest of it, it was like he was a Godsend, just amazing, he did everything.'

Lou would still have to write some songs for her to sing with the band, though. The results, rather incredibly, were some of the most affecting they would ever record, and quite unlike anything the group had yet attempted with any degree of sincerity: the beautiful, candlelit ballads 'Femme Fatale' (inspired by Warhol's suggestion that Lou write a song about Edie Sedgwick) and 'I'll Be Your Mirror' (written after Nico helped seduce Lou into letting her sing his songs with the line: 'Oh Lou, I'll be your mirror'), and another post-'Ostrich' wig-out, 'All Tomorrow's Parties', which Lou had already written but that in Nico's hands assumed real speed-comedown feeling. Her heavy German accent, ice-cold delivery – the epitome of the decadent dominatrix that had actually made her debut as a singer in December 1963 at New York's Blue Angel nightclub, where she blew the cobwebs off 'My Funny Valentine', turning it into a torch song for the genuinely suicidal – becoming just the latest, most sublime element of a sound already teetering between the screeching ballast of New York jazz experimentalism and filmic, monochrome European avant-gardism.

The first performance together as the Velvet Underground and Nico took place on 13 January 1966. It wasn't a Friday but it should have been. With the gleeful mischief of a master scene-setter, Warhol had arranged for the band to perform at a dinner for a psychiatrists' convention at a swanky hotel on Fifth Avenue. Again, Lou's instant reaction was to throw up his hands in horror. 'You've gotta be fucking kidding me!' But once Andy spelled out his plan Lou couldn't wait.

Warhol had been booked to give an after-dinner speech, which he convinced them to turn into a screening of one of his films, with a 'talk' afterwards. But as the dinner guests lit cigars and poured brandies in readiness at the end of their meals, the now darkened room was suddenly rent asunder by Barbara Rubin who burst through the doors wielding a movie-camera with an eye-searing bright light atop. At the same moment, the curtains parted to reveal the band launching into a monstrously loud 'Heroin', as Barbara raced between tables screaming provocatively about how big the men's penises were and how often they performed cunnilingus. Nico, standing imperiously on the stage staring into the darkness watched silently as the dozens of psychiatrists and their wives rapidly evacuated the scene of such terror. Andy was beside himself with glee. More so when the following day's edition of the *New York Times* ran a report under the headline: 'SHOCK TREATMENT FOR PSYCHIATRISTS!'

So began a blur of such events that would take the Velvet Underground – and Nico – on the trip of a lifetime as Andy Warhol's latest fad. The three months leading up to April, when they would go into a studio to record that first album, were like a Warhol film, but with a better narrative. Lou began an affair with Nico, whom Andy was also in love with, convinced she was the more beautiful embodiment of what he would have been had he been fortunate enough to be born a woman, and whom Cale affected not to be remotely interested in, amused at what he later called Lou's 'both consummated and constipated' relationship with the stone-faced ice-queen.

Andy took to filming the band in rehearsal at The Factory, footage from which he then put together as an hour-long movie titled *Symphony Of Sound*, one of the best records of that time and place, which can now be found on YouTube... Nico perched on a stool looking surprisingly self-conscious as she listlessly bangs a tambourine, never actually being given space for long enough to sing, amid a maelstrom of guitars, drums and Cale's horror-film viola, all four Velvets in shades, heads down, concentrating as they trundle through a 50-minute-plus instrumental improvisation, Nico smiling nervously down at her young blond son, Ari, then just four, sitting at her feet, looking lost until Nico hands him a maraca which he dutifully waves up and down, the most interesting moment near the end, after the cops seem to have put a stop to the row, and they are just standing around, until Nico touches Lou's arm, the signal for him to follow her out of the frame, Ari close behind.

Andy even began telling journalists that 'I don't really believe in painting any more' and that he was now more interested in finding a way of 'combining music, art and film all together'. In February, he put his money where his mouth was and booked the Velvet Underground into the Cinématèque for a week, in February, where he would put on his own version of the Piero Heliczer 'multi-media' event of the previous summer. Being Andy, of course, this would be much more spectacular, more innovative, more of a real art 'happening'. And it would be called: *Andy Warhol Uptight*.

The shows have since gone down in history. Picking up where the psychiatrist show left off, the band played, all in shades, they claimed, because of the bright psychedelic lights projected onto them but in reality because they looked cool, while Gerard Malanga stood on stage with them, lashing his whip and improvising dance moves to 'illustrate' the songs. Nico also stood on stage – no shades, just those deep swimming-pool eyes defying the gaze of the lights – but only sang the three songs they had written for her, as well as singing along, at one stage, to the record of Bob Dylan's 'I'll Keep It With Mine'. On top of all this Andy projected a selection of his short films, mainly the ones starring Edie Sedgwick, like *Screen Test No. 1* and *Beauty II*. Not everybody who was actually there liked it – including the band: Nico felt 'stupid'; Lou, still disgruntled at submitting centre-stage to Nico, was further put out with Malanga, who he thought also took away too much of the spotlight – but by the week's end apocryphal tales of people fainting during the show and others becoming so freaked out their lives changed overnight had turned it into a hit and the idea that Andy Warhol had his own rock group had taken hold.

Never one to waste time, the workaholic Warhol now booked them in for four days' recording at Scepter Studios on West 54th Street (the building to become famous in the 1970s for housing the infamous Studio 54 disco). With Andy splitting the costs – around $2000 – with the Columbia Records executive Norman Dolph, who engineered the sessions along with John Licata, the initial idea had been to shop the finished tapes to Columbia. But the know-betters at Columbia fobbed it off as some sort of artsy joke. The A&R geniuses at Atlantic Records and Elektra Records refused to take the tapes seriously either. Eventually a deal was done with the MGM-owned Verve Records, who had recently signed Frank Zappa's Mothers Of Invention. It was brokered by the same house producer, Tom Wilson, who had overseen five of Bob Dylan's earliest – and best – albums, as well as working on the first Mothers Of Invention album, *Freak Out!*, just weeks before. Wilson was less impressed by the Andy Warhol imprimatur that the package came with and more focused on three, as he saw it, potentially classic songs: 'I'm Waiting For The Man', 'Venus In Furs' and 'Heroin'. He insisted the band join him for two days at his favoured TTG studios in Los Angeles, where the songs were all re-recorded in May. A canny music biz veteran, Wilson still refused to sign off on the album until, as late as November 1966, they agreed to go back into the studio one last time – a Sunday when rates were cheap at Mayfair Studios in New York – to write and record what the producer considered a hit single: a self-consciously trite yet strangely affecting pop ditty they gave the throwaway title of 'Sunday Morning'. It was the most conventional-sounding, of-its-time recording the Velvet Underground would ever release, replete with Cale's tinkling celesta trickling like a stream over it. They were more than happy for Nico to sing it. Until, that is, Lou twigged it would be the band's next single. At which point he put his pointy leather boot down and insisted *he* sing it.

By then, Lou Reed had ingratiated himself further into Warhol's Factory scene as the Velvet Underground and Nico became the central focus of what Andy excitedly dubbed his Exploding Plastic Inevitable. Basically, an extension of the *Uptight* week at the Cinématèque, but taken to an even more illogical and fantastic climax, it began in April 1966, when Andy rented a Polish community hall, named the Dom, on St Mark's Place, in the boho East Village. For four weeks the Velvet Underground and Nico performed almost every night at the Dom, as Warhol flung more and yet more of his 'superstars', 'films', Factory 'friends' and anything else that crossed his amphetamine-fuelled mind at the stage as Lou and John, Sterling and Maureen did their best to keep playing. To highlight her importance in this 'performance piece', Nico would stand centre-stage, a living sculpture dressed in a white leather catsuit, as Lou, dressed all in black and still staring blankly from behind his shades, sang most of the songs but received the least attention. The back of the stage was also white, onto which Andy projected two of his films side by side, while out-front Malanga was back to dance with his whip, but joined this time by another Warhol actress, Mary Woronov. As if this were not enough, a giant mirror ball hung from the ceiling as Andy aimed strobe lights at the stage and the walls, sending those not already high on drugs into a psychological tailspin.

The shows even began to make money. Andy Warhol's *Uptight* had reportedly earned $12,000 over the course of its run. The EPI, as it became shortened to, reportedly brought in a healthy profit of over $18,000. Big numbers in 1966 for a band yet to actually release a record. Lou and the others were kept on war rations though, each given a five-dollar bill each day to keep them fed and watered. Any additional expenses – usually for drugs – would be diligently entered into a ledger. Sterling Morrison told Victor Bockris of seeing an entry in the ledger for five dollars' worth of heroin, and that when Warhol's accountant found it he gasped: 'What the hell is this?'

When it was over the band was famous – on the New York art scene, at least – but Lou was unhappy. The way the shows were received you'd think Nico and Gerard Malanga were the stars. Their only review in a mainstream media outlet, the *New York Times*, appeared on the women's page. Some nights they were set upon by drunken, drug-crazed loons offended by how 'obscene' the show was. Lou's jealousy of Nico boiled over into constant personal barbs, freezing her out in favour of the street hustlers and male groupies of the after-hours Village clubs the band would end up in, after the show was over but the methedrine was still burning through the singer's synapses. Now living in a loft on Grand Street, in the then still-seedy SoHo district of Lower Manhattan, Lou was building his own entourage of acolytes and followers. He knew he still needed Andy but was ready to wash his hands of Nico, and pissed off with the seemingly more calm, self-assured Cale, who began to attract more serious attention.

Yet these would prove, in retrospect, to be the best days of the Velvet Underground. At a residency that summer at The Trip, in Los Angeles, they had intended to reproduce the EPI spectacle and hoped for it to be received perhaps even more warmly in the land of sleazy Hollywood tricks and dicks than it had been even in hard-assed New York. Yet they could not have been more wrong.

Songs such as the blood-pounding 'I'm Waiting For The Man', with its site-specific references to streets like Lexington Avenue, in which the protagonist, a not even thinly veiled Lou Reed, would wait for his dealer, 'twenty-six dollars in my hand', and the equally psychotic-sounding 'Run, Run, Run', with its tawdry tale of selling your soul on 'a walk down to Union Square', had held a dusty mirror up to New York's Lower East Side sensibilities, but in LA, where the sun always shone and everyone travelled in an open-top car, they made no sense at all. Worse, at a time when the West Coast was awash with groups singing about the virtues of love-love-love and the deeply meaningful joys of LSD, songs like 'Heroin' – 'It's my life and it's my wife,' droned Lou – and 'The Black Angel's Death Song' – more droning from Lou, this time about 'bleeding razors' on an 'old city street in the East – were merely seen as downers. Even ostensibly straight rockers like 'There She Goes Again', with its massive pop chorus and rich Byrds-style chords, was belied by its dark denouement: 'You better hit her.' These Velvet Underground motherfuckers looked like a bunch of junkies and fags, what did they have to do with wearing flowers in your hair and loving the one you're with? Night creatures squirming beneath the pulsing neon ooze of Sunset Boulevard, the quicker they slunk back to whatever busted New York fire hydrant they'd spurted from the better.

Reed, for his part, despised the West Coast scene and what he saw as their pompous, wrongheaded, tedious culture. As far as Lou was concerned, the difference between what he and the Velvets were doing and what, on paper, might have been thought of as fellow-counterculture-travellers like The Doors and the Grateful Dead were up to was the difference between soft drugs and hard, with no confusion over which Reed and the Velvets stood for. Or as he put it in 2003: 'Well, we were also really, really smart and the [West Coast hippy] stuff was really, really stupid.' He scowled. 'It was purely a matter of brains.'

The two-week residency at The Trip ended after just three days. But while LA luminaries like Cher made a big deal of walking out on the first night, famously declaring that the only thing this kind of music would replace would be suicide, others in the audience were genuinely intrigued, not least the 23-year-old Jim Morrison, though in his case, as with so many others at the time, his attention was more focused on Malanga, who danced in a Marlon Brando T-shirt, lifting toy barbells. During 'Heroin' he pretended to shoot up with a giant syringe then lit candles. Morrison was so wowed he co-opted Gerard's antics into his own stage act, and later had his own short-lived but self-destructive affair with Nico.

The LA misadventure would be repeated to a greater or lesser extent at every stop the Velvet Underground made outside New York. When they appeared on the same bill at the Fillmore Ballroom in San Francisco – still under the EPI umbrella – as Zappa and the Mothers, Lou was scornful of both Zappa and the acid-drenched audience that made it clear how much they preferred his freak-power musical melodrama to the Velvets' gutter rock. He began to question what they were even doing performing alongside such hippies.

As Lou recalled for Bruce Pollock: 'Ralph Gleason, the dean of American reviewers, wrote in a review, I'll never forget it; he said the whole love thing going on in San Francisco has been partially sabotaged by the influx of this trash from New York, representing everything they had cured.' He added with a sneer: 'They thought acid was going to solve everything... We just said bullshit, you people are fucked. That's not the way it is and you're kidding yourselves. And they hated us.'

Lou was far more put out though when, having ended up in hospital after he nearly paralysed himself on a particularly toxic shot of meth, he awoke to find the band and Angus MacLise standing around his bed, the latter invited back by Cale to stand in on drums, with Moe moving to bass, while Sterling took over guitar and John and Nico took over the singing, for a show in Chicago. Lou was horrified. Sure that MacLise must now regret having walked out on them, Lou left Angus in no doubt that however ill he was this would be a strictly *temporary* arrangement.

It seemed that, for Lou Reed, every success would come with a condition attached, some bleak reminder that no matter what his new friends at The Factory thought of him, he was underneath it all the same vulnerable, nervy mother's boy, trying to straighten his hair and hide behind his permanent midnight shades. The same month, July, when the first Velvet Underground single was pressed up and sent out to various radio stations – an early rougher version of 'All Tomorrow's Parties' – his former mentor, Delmore Schwartz, was found dead in a dingy downtown New York hotel room. He was just 52 and had died of a heart attack. It was two days before anyone came forward to identify the body. Lou would later ensure the track 'European Son' – a ten-line poem that is quickly subsumed into six minutes of La Monte Young-style noise-chaos of guitar feedback, cleaving viola, thrumming bass and manic disjointed drums which closed the first Velvets album – was dedicated on the sleeve to Delmore.

It was the same when the *Velvet Underground & Nico* album was finally released, in March 1967. Lou and John and Andy and everybody else at The Factory not busy being bored doing something else knew it was an instant classic. Everyone else outside The Factory, including the band's record company, had other ideas though. Which only made Lou angrier, only made him hurt more, but at the same time even more proud that at least Andy was there to believe in them.

He recalled how the suits at Verve had tried to insist they remove all the 'dirty words'. How Andy pulled Lou aside and told him: '"Whatever you do don't clean it up, don't slick it up, don't let them change anything, do it exactly the way you've been doing it." And he made sure that happened, because he was there. I mean they [the record company] wouldn't even talk to us. They talked to him: they said: "Mr Warhol, blah, blah, blah." And he would say' – adopting an uncannily accurate Warhol voice – '"Oh, that's great", and that would be that. They'd look at him, because however strange they thought we were, Andy with a silver wig? Right to the head of the class, you know, and he would be really, really aggressively fey on purpose. You know, really push it at them. If you look at pictures where everybody posed for pictures Andy would do something really odd or something, so you look at that picture, you have to look at *him*. And when you were with these people they had to go to him. None of [them] was wearing a silver wig.'

Things got back on track when they found themselves playing in Detroit along with the English pop fops the Yardbirds. Andy announced he would officiate at the (mock) wedding of two of the superstars, out in a windy Michigan field. At the same time the band's tour manager began pounding on a car with a sledgehammer, not stopping until it was crushed into flat, mangled smithereens. The Yardbirds couldn't quite believe what was happening.

Famously credited as producer on the album sleeve – a claim Tom Wilson always disputed, insisting that if anything it was John Cale who had been the real musical director of the album – where Warhol really did score as the record's producer, said Lou, was in how he protected the group, from the record company, from the critics, all of whom were openly hostile, from their own self-doubts and fears, even when they were tangled up in a morass of drug comedowns and sex-treachery.

Andy was their protector, said Lou. 'We were so nothing, what was there to criticise with us? No one ever heard of us. You can't criticise a zero, you know, so they criticised him. He could care less.' Lou learned more from this so-called 'failure', he would later conjecture, than he ever would have had the album been embraced by the rock press. Just being around Warhol was worth all the good reviews in the world, he said. 'I watched. I watched everything he did, and I studied everything he did, and I really listened to him because he's so smart. But, I mean smart and *does* things, not just theoretical smart, like smart and he's right out there – one idea after another. People were like: "How can he produce the record? He's not a musician."'

People were stupid. How many times did Lou have to tell 'em?

3
Light And Dark

The release in 1967 of *The Velvet Underground & Nico* may historically have been the beginning of a brilliant musical story, but it also spelled the end of Andy Warhol's patronage of both Lou Reed and the band he now seemed determined to turn into a mainstream success.

For Lou, Andy was 'a magnificent creature, and he really thought about it. Just look at the way he was before he switched over from commercial art. It's one of the great ideas, and boom, he just goes and does it. And he would put his money where his mouth was; all the movies, the this-and-that were funded by him out of his own money. And he wasn't getting anything back out of it. When I left, I just left. He didn't say: "Hey, I've done this and that for you I want twenty per cent for ever" or anything. He was really noble.'

Well, that may have been how Lou Reed liked to remember it when he spoke those words in 2003. But the truth was much more prosaic. Not very noble at all, in fact. As far as the music business was concerned, Andy was as inexperienced as Lou. He may have conjured up what is now considered one of the most iconic album sleeves in the history of rock – the yellow banana on the white background that originally came as a peel-off sticker, and Andy's famous autograph mimeographed beneath – but he remained blissfully unconcerned with commonplaces like royalty rates of record sales, or marketing and promotion budgets, tour booking and the rest of the day-to-day palaver of managing a rock act. Warhol saw the Velvet Underground as simply another branch of his own artistic empire. Now they were up and running with an album out and concert bookings though, contracts would have to be signed. Warhol and his business manager, Paul Morrissey, saw it simply: all monies accrued by the group would come to Andy's company, Warvel, which Morrissey had set up specifically for the purpose, with Andy retaining 25 per cent before passing on the remaining 75 per cent to the group. Lou, though, had a better idea. The band would receive all monies, and pass on Andy's 25 per cent to him.

Morrissey thought the idea stank, reasoning, not unjustly, that without Warhol's name and direct involvement, the Velvet Underground would still be scrabbling around begging for scraps. Andy, who didn't disagree but hated confrontation, grudgingly agreed. But things would never be the same between him and Lou again. Though the pair would ostensibly remain on good terms, Lou and the Velvets were now effectively on their own. There would be no Warhol silkscreens of Lou Reed. No chic portraits or invitations to parties.

Andy would live up to the nickname Lou and John and the others had given him behind his back – Drella, a conflation of Cinderella and Dracula, reflecting his you-shall-go-to-the-ball celebrity-lust and his other side, the vampiric figure who devoured the personalities of those that wasped into his orbit until he'd sucked them dry and abandoned them. Lou would move the band out of The Factory and into their own rehearsal space in Broome Street, as he began to finally take over as leader. They completed another week-long engagement as the EPI at the Dom, but by April Nico was on her way out too, recording her own album for Verve with Tom Wilson. Titled *Chelsea Girls*, not coincidentally the same title as the Warhol film she had just finished starring in, and featuring songs written for her by newer lovers like Jackson Browne and (it was whispered behind Lou's back) John Cale, as well as those songs Lou and John and Sterling would grant her almost as a parting gift, it was the beginning of a career for Nico that Lou was now paranoid might eclipse his own.

In May, the final EPI show took place at Steve Paul's Scene – the small but increasingly hip Manhattan club, which The Doors would also make their home-from-home that summer and where Jimi Hendrix would make his New York debut a month later. Lou did not shed any tears. 'It was a show by and for freaks,' he would insist to Bruce Pollock, 'of which there turned out to be many more than anyone had suspected, who finally had a place to go where they wouldn't be hassled and where they could have a good time.' He added: 'The people who showed up – everybody just looked at everybody else and said: "Wow, there are a lot of us." So we knew they were there.' Now, though, he was impatient to move on, to be taken more seriously as a rock artist, not just another one of Andy's freaks.

By July, Nico was hanging out at the Monterey Pop Festival with Brian Jones, and Lou and the Velvets were playing an extended run at a journeyman rock club in Philadelphia called The Trauma. The Velvet Underground, onstage at least, were now having to slum it like all the other rock wannabes. A fact brought home with a deflating bump when they appeared at Poor Richard's in Chicago that month. The band had been booked on the understanding that Andy Warhol would be also be coming to town, and the club's owners had set up a string of local TV and radio interviews to publicise the gig. But Andy didn't show up – sending Brigid Polk dressed in a white suit instead, to pass herself off as Andy; disappointment turned to outright hostility as the band ploughed on regardless in an unventilated room with temperatures now soaring to 106 degrees Fahrenheit.

'God, you get out on the road into these towns with one television station. Merv Griffin. You get so sick for New York,' Lou moaned to Robert Greenfield. 'You have to grab a copy of *Vogue*...'

Things were becoming drab, predictable. Andy was no longer on the end of the phone when they needed him and Nico was now shacked up with Jim Morrison, whose band, The Doors, had the No. 1 of the summer with 'Light My Fire', and who was helping her write songs for her second album. Lou began to feel his career wasn't being handled well enough. When a minor Factory face named Eric Emerson decided to sue MGM-Verve for the 'illegitimate' use of his photo on the back sleeve of the Velvets album, Lou was incensed that Andy didn't deal with him personally, instead allowing Verve to take the album out of circulation for six weeks while they airbrushed his image from the cover; it effectively killed the album as a commercial proposition. Finally, at a tense meeting between Lou and Andy backstage at a club in Boston called the Boston Tea Party, where Andy and Nico had arrived – surprise, surprise – only for Lou to refuse to allow Nico anywhere near the stage, and to inform a for once far from passive Andy, afterwards, that his services were no longer required, it was over.

Warhol's coterie of hangers-on would always maintain that it was simply a natural parting of the ways that Warhol would sooner or later encourage all his apron-string artists to make. But this was the first time any of them had actually walked away from Warhol without being shown the door first. For the rest of his life, Reed would maintain that Warhol was shocked and angry at the news. What nobody in the Warhol camp yet realised was that Lou had already made his move, agreeing to sign the band to a management contract with a 'real' music-biz mover and shaker named Steve Sesnick – co-owner, in fact, of the Boston Tea Party.

Steve was everything that Andy was not. He had first-hand knowledge of the music business as it was rapidly developing in America in the mid-1960s, he understood record contracts, how to book tours. He was always available whenever Lou phoned to ask the dozens of questions he always had about how everything worked and, most important, how everyone got paid and how much. For all his protestations about not caring about money, Lou was in thrall to Sesnick's talk of the riches that could be made from singing and playing the guitar. It didn't matter that John Cale took the opposite view of Sesnick's appointment, fretting that Lou was forgetting 'what our original precepts were,' as he confided to Victor Bockris. Or that Moe laughed at Steve's ability to talk everything up, telling her the Velvets would soon be as big as The Beatles.

The only thing still going somewhere interesting and new for the Velvet Underground was the music. With Lou and John no longer constrained by the multi-media shebang Warhol had insisted on they now immersed themselves more fiercely than ever in the music they were making, improvising madly at every show, giving scant regard to how much the audience might be 'enjoying' the spectacle. This was no longer about engaging the whole room in an 'experience' so much as about returning to the experimental values Reed and Cale had originally conceived of before Andy Warhol had subsumed them into becoming one more bizarre flesh-and-blood product of his endlessly churning Factory.

The results, recorded back at Mayfair in the second week of September 1967, again with Tom Wilson at the controls, were at once smoother than the first VU album yet equally adventurous. Less immediately shocking yet actually more daring. Mayfair was known for its advanced eight-track studios – this at a time when even The Beatles were still using four-track recording facilities – and the Velvets, with Wilson's help, for the first time used the studio to its full advantage. So that while the title track – 'White Light/White Heat', a two-and-a-half minute clamour of door-banging drums, pounding piano and sneering vocals, not dissimilar to 'Waiting For The Man', only this time the drug under inspection is pure white pharmaceutical speed – and 'I Heard Her Call My Name' – another methedrine-spike of feedback and hollow backing vocals (like the Beach Boys if they'd been dead for three days) – were sharply redolent of the first VU album, what most characterised the second VU album was its willingness to outgrow its artsy primitivism as it strived for a new musical plateau.

This is best conveyed on the album's two longest tracks. Firstly, the eight-minute 'The Gift', which comprises two separate yet conjoined strands. One, the music, a solid groove of splintered guitars and humming bass and drums, emanating from the right-hand stereo speaker; the other, a short story written by Lou when he was at Syracuse and recited in spoken-word form by Cale, emanating from the left-hand speaker. It tells the comically dark tale of one Waldo Jeffers, who has been separated from his girlfriend, Marsha Bronson, for 'more than two months' and, reaching 'his limit', decides to mail himself to her, special delivery. It all comes to a predictably grisly end, of course, yet the story is almost beside the point. In an age when most record-buyers still owned mono players, this was rock thinking several steps ahead.

In a similarly literary vein is the track that immediately follows on the album, 'Lady Godiva's Operation'. Built on the bed of another finger-snapping groove, it's another story – no verses or chorus, with Cale again handling the vocals in a soft almost spoken-word style, which Reed then begins to interject into – based on the legend of the famous English lady who rode naked through the streets of Coventry, but here becomes a predator of 'every poor daughter's son' forced to undergo a brain operation, which the doctor botches, leaving Godiva screaming back into semi-consciousness.

It was the album's closing track, though, that would stand, as it continues to do today, almost a half-century later, as one of the great landmark moments in both the story of Lou Reed and the Velvet Underground and the whole history of rock and whatever you wish to call the thing that is not rock at all but something that exists somewhere in its own universe.

From its disorienting title – 'Sister Ray', an unheard of confluence of the male and female, shocking on the eye and ear of a society still unaccustomed to such 'perverted' concepts as cross-pollinating sexuality – to its woozy, falling-out-of-your-seat fairground ride of crunching, whining guitars, brutal, face-slapping drums and truly nightmarish phantom-of-the-opera keyboards, supplied by Cale by running the organ through a distorted guitar amp, this was a frighteningly strange new realm of rock music no one even knew existed before, let alone attempted to explore. Recorded in one continuous take that finally sputters out of life after 17 minutes like a twitching corpse, 'Sister Ray' was the band's new magnum opus, a musical Frankenstein's monster built from dead parts out on the road in the summer of 1967, in the wake of Andy's limp-wristed departure and Steve Sesnick's fast-talking, money-down arrival.

The lyrics are superb. Cut-ups of scenes Lou had witnessed first hand throughout his time first as narrow-eyed Warhol Factory acolyte then as speed-junkie poet of the blood-strewn, sperm-encrusted lofts and alleyways of New York's cheap-seats neighbourhoods where drugs and money and sex and murder were all but interchangeable on any given night of the rotten nowhere-left-to-go week. Populated by pipe-cooking sailors in pink leather and he-she couples searching for their mainline and sucking on their ding-dongs as one of them complains of stains on the carpet from where a body just fell shot through the head – 'And by the way have you got a dollar?' This was a Fellini film spied throughout the bleached-out lens of a Warhol movie that doesn't know how to end and doesn't care. By the time the *White Light/White Heat* album was released in January 1968, 'Sister Ray' had assumed even more monstrous form out on the road, blasting uncomprehending audiences for up to 40 minutes. They had also added a sort of overture, which they titled 'Sweet Sister Ray'; this alone would often go on for over half an hour.

Strange to relate then that the song which would most clearly signpost where the Velvets would go next with their music was the almost somnambulant 'Here She Comes Now', which closed side one. A gorgeously wayward ditty written by Lou, John and Sterling, about love and orgasm condensed into just six lines repeated over a bossa nova rhythm, it was slight but not fey, feminine but butch. Who knew that this would be the key to the future of the Velvet Underground, as they finally left behind the art galleries and S&M salons in order to fully embrace the kind of fame and fortune to be found out on the road of the established rock clubs and pop radio that Steve Sesnick had convinced Lou Reed – still eager to believe in a better future – was there for the taking?

Maybe it was this that caused him to shudder so when Lou read the reviews, such that there were, of *White Light/White Heat*, peppered as they were again with the words 'obscene' and 'shocking'. In conversation about it with the famed rock biographer Barney Hoskyns almost 30 years later, Lou was still fuming. 'Lyrically, I don't think there was too much else apart from Dylan and the Velvets that was engaging that part of your head,' he reasoned. 'Which made it so absurd to be told you were doing something shocking.' Compared, he said, with adjacent literature of the time like Allen Ginsberg's poem *Howl* and William Burroughs's *Naked Lunch*, 'There was such a narrow-minded view of what a song could be. And I'd have to sit there with people saying, "Don't you feel guilty for glamorising heroin, for all the people who've shot up drugs because of you?" I get that to this day, even though I didn't notice a drop-off in the sales of narcotics when I stopped taking drugs.'

Lou and the Velvets now sacrificed themselves to the rock'n'roll treadmill, playing the same places The Doors and Creedence Clearwater Revival were playing – the Boston Tea Party, Chicago's Kinetic Ballroom, San Francisco's Avalon Ballroom, La Cave in Cleveland – on and on throughout the early months of 1968. But despite accruing reviews of the standard set by the local freak rag in Chicago, which wrote of the band taking 'everyone ten miles high on their unique hard rock sound', still their records didn't sell. The title track to *White Light/White Heat* had been released as a promo single to radio at the tail end of '67 but received next to no play. When the album was released in January, it received an official 'ban' on greater New York radio – an insult that caused Lou to vow he would never play the city again, which he kept to until 1970 – and consequently fared even worse in the US charts than had its predecessor, barely scraping in at No. 199.

This was not how Steve had said it would be. In New York, Lou was still considered a star, not least in the backroom of his new favourite hangout, Max's Kansas City, the late-night club on the corner of Park Avenue South and 17th Street that

Andy had introduced him to back when they were still more than just good friends. Owned by the underground art world scene-maker and restaurateur Mickey Ruskin, Max's became both a regular gig for the Velvets and a place where, in the backroom, usually presided over by Andy and his entourage, Lou and his drag queen, junkie, muso, actor, sex-worker friends could relax and be whichever self they had decided on that week. Here was where you could find up-and-comers like Alice Cooper slumped at a table next to Edie Sedgwick, Jim Morrison standing at the bar getting a blowjob from two chicks at the same time, while Andy looked on and fidgeted with lust, Gregory Corso raging at anyone who was foolish enough to come too close that they were 'fakes!', or William Burroughs nodding off next to Allen Ginsberg, who was busy trying to make conversation with Factory drag queens like Candy Darling. Here was where you could talk trash, shoot speed, smoke smack, smash glasses on the floor and forget you lived in an unheated dump over on West Third Street, like Lou and John and Sterling did.

Around the rest of the country though, the Velvet Underground may as well have not existed, so little were their name or music in circulation. When an infuriated Lou pestered Steve Sesnick with what he should do, Steve shrugged and suggested he look closer to home for the solution to his problems. Maybe the band was simply too out there, he seemed to suggest, too artsy and pretentious – too much about John Cale and not enough about its true star, Lou Reed.

By the summer of 1968, the four members of the Velvet Underground had separated and were all living away from each other. John had moved into the Chelsea Hotel, where he was now heavily involved with another Warhol starlet and future clothes designer, Betsey Johnson. Lou had moved into another shithole loft in the Village with just his guitars and a bed to keep him company. He didn't really know or care where Sterling and Moe might be, referring to the Velvets now as 'my band', just a bunch of sidemen extras in the rapidly flickering movie unspooling in his dragged-out, drugged-up mind.

With Sesnick now setting the agenda with Lou, Cale began to fight back – literally on more than one occasion, drunkenly attacking Lou and putting the rest of the band on an edge they would never finally climb down from. For John, this was about a battle for the very soul of the Velvet Underground. For Lou, this was about fulfilling his dreams of rock stardom, pure and simple, before the chance was gone, as Steve told him it would be if he didn't make the most of his opportunities now while they still could.

A nadir was reached with the next recording sessions that were booked, where Steve had agreed with Lou that they would record some material which would finally get them onto the radio: proper singles material, for which Lou, who found he liked writing to a brief and a deadline, came up with two appropriately innocuous-sounding tracks: 'Ferryboat Bill' and 'Temptation Inside Your Heart'. Both tracks were lightweight compared to anything on the first two VU albums, but no less admirable for that. The problem was, they still sounded like the side-of-the-mouth creations of a know-better New Yorker pandering to the pop crowd than they did the genuine article; an in-joke the intended audience wouldn't get, let alone find amusing. John, meanwhile, in a trade-off of now overtly clashing sensibilities, insisted on them recording his own latest contribution, an instrumental viola-drone, with the surely ironically jolly title 'Hey Mr Rain'. In the end none of these tracks was released by Verve, who were now starting to question whether the band was taking the job in hand seriously enough.

When John married Betsey in April, it drove a further rift between him and Lou, who was madly jealous. Lately Lou seemed to have lost his taste for sexual partners, repelling the advances of both men and women; the others merely assumed he was now so deep into his drugs and his rock star trip that he simply had no time to love anybody but himself. It wasn't true. In fact, Lou was secretly seeing his old flame from Syracuse, the beautiful Shelley Albin. Shelley was now married and had moved with her husband to New York in 1966, since which time Lou and she had begun seeing each other again but only – much to Lou's disappointment – as 'good friends'. By 1968, however, the rumour was that this friendship had blossomed once again into a full-blown love affair. Certainly, Lou would claim so, to friends, and by mentioning his love for someone who was married in song.

'Lou and I connected when we were too young to really put it into words,' she would recall years later. But, though she loved his fierce intelligence, his flare for the extraordinary bon mot or surprisingly romantic gesture, Shelley had always been wary of what she saw as his 'crazy side'. And the more he begged her to leave her husband and come and have a real life with him, the more she shrunk from the idea, unwilling to become seduced like everyone else in his orbit seemed to be, by his genius, his music, his poetry and his ultra-demanding personality, his sheer determination to make it, one way or the other. No matter how hard he implored, insulting her, accusing her of choosing 'security' over 'love', Shelley refused to leave her husband, even if Lou was right about the last part.

Abject at his failure to win Shelley over, increasingly impatient and angry over John's resistance to his and Steve's plans for rock'n'roll immortality, Lou arrived for the latest round of Velvet Underground shows on the West Coast in June, with his mind whirring. Then something happened that would bring everything else into sharp relief. On his way to breakfast one morning at his hotel with Steve Sesnick, they glanced at a stack of newspapers, on which a headline announced that Andy Warhol had been shot and was now fighting for his life in hospital in New York. The would-be assassin: another disaffected Factory reject named Valerie Solanas.

Lou didn't know what to do, how best to react. Should he phone? Should he jump on the first plane back? But, as Steve reminded him, he had been out of Andy's loop for some time now, and they still had another three months' worth of shows out on the coast to get through. Lou stayed on. The band continued their schedule through shows in San Francisco, San Diego, Los Angeles and back up the coast to Vancouver, then Philadelphia and, finally, Boston, where, on 28 September 1968, John Cale played his last show as a member of the Velvet Underground.

Since Andy's shooting, which he now, miraculously, appeared to be slowly recovering from, Lou's attitude had hardened towards both Cale and his own career. Lou felt John was now in the way, blocking his every move to make the band more able to become viable commercially, and still retain a sense of originality. Steve was getting them some well-paid gigs, sometimes as much as $2,500 a night. Sometimes, though, it was still as little as just $600. They needed to make the leap to the next level. But Lou felt he couldn't have that kind of conversation with John. He had never felt so thwarted, so near to and yet so far from making it. Finally, it was decided one night, as Lou and Steve stayed up late as usual after a show plotting, John would have to go. Lou presented his decision to Sterling and Moe at a secret band meeting – to which John was not invited – as a fait accompli. Either they fired John or Lou would split the band. Sterling and Moe eventually agreed, but never got over it. Sterling, in particular, never forgave Lou.

When John received the news – delivered by Sterling, at Lou's insistence, as he was simply too scared to do the dirty himself – he did not go quietly. Things had lately reached an all-time low between them, he acknowledged, but the manner of his sacking – 'all done by sleight of hand' – left a bad taste in his mouth – 'treason!' – that would never quite go away. For John, who had been Lou's musical partner in the Velvet Underground project from day one, it only rubbed salt into the wound when Sesnick then issued a press statement announcing his departure, quoting Lou as saying how fervently he hoped that 'one day John will be recognised as... the Beethoven of his day'.

John Cale's replacement in the Velvet Underground was a 21-year-old bassist, Doug Yule. Doug gave Lou Reed everything that Cale could not; a solid if unspectacular player who looked up to Lou and did everything he was told. Introduced by Steve Sesnick, who knew him from Boston, where he had been the bassist in a well-regarded local outfit called The Glass Menagerie, overnight Doug became almost a Lou Reed mini-me. Out on the road with the band in October, just a week after landing the gig, by the time the band fetched up at TTG Studios in Hollywood, in November, to make their first album with the new line-up, Doug was dressing like Lou, singing like Lou, and shutting up whenever Lou wanted him to. From Long Island, like Lou, too, Doug was simply happy to be the sideman Steve and Lou now craved. His reward: to sing the opening track – because Lou told him to – on what would be another remarkable Velvet Underground album, if one entirely unlike anything they had done before: the so syrupy it almost chokes you 'Candy Says', aka Candy Darling, late of Warhol's Factory and, four years later, properly immortalised in the song that would finally win Lou that elusive hit: 'Walk On The Wild Side'.

Working on what would be the most low-key album Lou Reed would ever make, Lou had never been happier. Still seeing Shelley Albin on the side, he had also begun a less furtive relationship with the Warhol Factory manager, Billy Name. Billy it was who had cradled Andy while they waited for the ambulance after the Solanas shooting; Billy who 'silversided' the Factory and was in command of its day-to-day running during Warhol's craziest years. Billy who'd had a brief fling with Andy and probably best understood why Lou had to leave when he did, whether he personally agreed with his reasons or not. And it was Billy now who offered Lou the most comfort and companionship as he set out to remake the Velvet Underground entirely in his own fractured image.

It's all there on the finished recording: an endless parade of the most personal love songs, or songs about love, Lou Reed would ever write and sing. And though it remains somewhat further down the highbrow critical pantheon than either of the first two, mind-blistering VU albums, the album they simply called *The Velvet Underground* would become many people's favourite.

Having things his own way at last certainly brought out a surprisingly soft side to Lou Reed's work. The aforementioned opener, 'Candy Says', is so delicate it almost breaks at its spindly climax, when Doug almost whispers the line, 'What do you think I'd see, if I could walk away from... me?'

'Some Kind Of Love' is about Billy *and* Shelley, Lou expounding the then – yes – shocking idea that there might be more than one kind of love, though none was greater than any other. Imagine? While 'Pale Blue Eyes', one of most fragile and heartrending songs ever written, is solely about Shelley. How happy, sad, mad and bad she makes him feel, sometimes all at once, and how despite it all she remains 'my mountain top, my peak'. All this sung in a low candlelit voice with guitars that smoulder like cigarettes glowing in the dark.

The most surprising, unnerving, yet transcendental moment of all, though, is the track that follows, 'Jesus'. With its hymnal wish for Jesus to help Lou find his 'proper place' lest he fall further from grace, the only instruments the gently murmuring acoustic and electric guitars of Lou and Sterling, Doug Yule's baby-Lou voice harmonising like the play of light on a bedsheet, there is nothing put on or freaked out going on here, the real shock being the feeling of love it arouses, whichever crosses one has to bear.

It's the same with the uplifting 'I'm Set Free', another shadow-song set aglow by the breathtaking message it seems to want to preach loud and clear as a bell, Lou down on his knees testifying, no less, as the marching chorus, Moe's drums like Spectre's on 'You've Lost That Lovin' Feeling', builds to the Zen-like denouement: Lou set free... 'to find a new illusion'.

It sounds doe-eyed and impossibly righteous. The sound of a sorry-arsed sinner repenting, and for once it seems that's exactly what it is: no more veils of irony and disdain to hide behind, no more knife-sharp words to tear at your preconceptions or sneeringly shove their ding-dongs in your face, just impure, non-virginal, compromised, yet all the more breathtaking for it, love sweet love.

There are even gently comedic moments like 'That's The Story Of My Life', where Lou ponders the difference between wrong and right while pointing out that Billy Name, whom he name-checks, 'says both those words are dead', and strumming the kind of semi-acoustic guitar last heard on the most charming of those early Beatles tunes like 'I'm A Loser' or 'Eight Days A Week'. While the album closes with 'Afterhours', a kind of punk 'Baby It's Cold Outside', sung deliciously by Moe Tucker, who belies the song's deliberately syrupy toy-shop acoustic by singing Lou's words about closing the door and making the night last for ever with almost hypnotic conviction, clearly his idea of what staying at home with your one true love – or in his case two – should be all about.

Even the two rockers on the album – the bone-rattling 'What Goes On' and the lush folk rock of 'Beginning To See

The Light' – are preoccupied with love and the promise of salvation. The title of the latter says it all, the joyful celebration of guitars that accompanies it undeniable. While the latter outs it even more simply, reassuring the lady that as long as she 'be good' and do what she should, 'You know it'll be all right!'

The only exception, and a track that would have sat easily on either of the first VU albums, is the wonderfully bizarre near nine-minute opus, 'The Murder Mystery', which, somewhat like 'The Gift' from *White Light/White Heat*, uses the new stereo technology to conjure up an audio experiment of cinematic proportions. It features all four band members' voices, but most prominently Lou's and Sterling's, who recite from a complete story, panned over both left- and right-hand speakers, as the band churn away in the background like a hungry stomach. The effect is pleasingly eerie, wondrously innovative, yet strangely listenable, and the only track that John Cale would conceivably have been proud of.

Released in March 1969, at Sesnick's insistence on the mainstream MGM label, as opposed to the 'experimental' Verve imprint, *The Velvet Underground*, despite its much lighter touch and more universal lyrical themes, would have one overriding thing in common with its full-velocity predecessors: it was the most tremendous commercial flop. Even as it was picking up the best record reviews the Velvet Underground had yet had – Robert Christgau, the doyen of music critics, gave it a big thumbs-up in the *Village Voice*, praising it as 'tuneful, well-written, exceptionally well sung' though demurring, predictably, at the 'bummer experiment' of 'The Murder Mystery'; Lester Bangs, destined to become Lou's nemesis in the rock press throughout the 1970s, reviewing it in *Rolling Stone* also professed a strong dislike for 'The Murder Mystery' and, more mysteriously, the effervescent 'Pale Blue Eyes', but concluded that the album as a whole would be the one to at last convince the naysayers that Lou and the Velvets could 'write and play any kind of music they want to with equal brilliance' – the album was already tumbling from its humble perch of No. 197, back down to nothing. While the single chosen to supposedly ignite the flames, 'What Goes On', was once again completely ignored even by the then newly emerging FM stations so besotted with the 'album-oriented' music of other coming American giants like the Airplane and Dead, Love and The Doors.

For Lou, it was the beginning of the end of his belief in the Velvet Underground, of the promises of Steve Sesnick, even the love of Billy and Shelley. Nobody could ever save him. Now he was sure. Though of course whenever anybody dared to bring up the subject of his latest commercial failure he was instantly defiant, unshakable in his beliefs that he had always made the right move, no matter what John and Andy and Nico or anyone else had to say or thought about it.

It really didn't matter that *The Velvet Underground* had failed in the charts. It really didn't. Lou was sure. He told everybody.

4
Unloaded

Nineteen sixty-nine was supposed to be the best year yet for Lou Reed's Velvet Underground, the start of big things. In fact, the story was now drawing to an ignominious close; the year ending as it had begun, with Lou still hoping for, no longer expecting, some kind of commercial breakthrough. Except now he no longer had the clammy embrace of artistic validation that being a favoured son of Andy Warhol had previously afforded him. Three flop albums in a row, no interest whatsoever in their singles from radio, and only the half-promise of a final fling at chart acceptance with an album Lou would build like a glorified remnant from his Jades days left the Velvet Underground adrift in a world where they were now considered little more than a curiosity. This was the year of both Woodstock and Altamont – the year when the psychedelic hippy rock dream, as espoused in August on the muddy fields of upstate New York, would be transformed into the all too real nightmare of a bleak racetrack in Oakland where Hell's Angels would terrorise and eventually slay one of a Rolling Stones crowd.

Yet the Velvet Underground would not find a place in either narrative. In fact, they were going in exactly the opposite direction. The dark overlords of New York's gutter state at a time when the rest of rock was busy putting flowers in its hair, now things were finally turning ugly the Velvet Underground were being led by Lou towards their prettiest, most appealing music yet. Wrong and wrong again.

Still slogging around on the conventional rock circuit, in the forlorn hope that the new *The Velvet Underground* album might pick up some traction, Lou was caught between doing the right thing and hating himself for it. When Steve Sesnick booked the Velvet Underground into gigs like the one they did in February, at the Stanley Theater in Pittsburgh, opening the show for The Fugs and the Grateful Dead, Lou dug that this was Steve doing what a top rock biz guy should for his band. But no one seemed to be getting it any more. A review of the show in the local underground music sheet, the *Pittsburgh Point*, spoke volumes of the world they were now trying to live in. 'The Velvet Underground was more velvet than underground – smooth, soft, and sensuous. The juxtaposition of "What Goes On In Your Mind" [*sic*] to a "Merry Melodies" cartoon (starring Bugs, would you believe, Bunny) rearranged our brainwaves in nostalgic patterns.'

Even then the places they played and how often they played them made the whole thing seem barely worthwhile. In the 273 days between January and September 1969 the Velvet Underground did just 44 shows – and 15 of those were at Sesnick's own Boston Tea Party venue, with another six at the Woodrose Ballroom, the other regular club venue in Massachusetts. Some of the gigs weren't even at rock clubs. They were at basketball gyms (Washington University, in May), local fund-raising events (a benefit for the Mason Fire Fighters in New Hampshire, in August), tiny wooden huts where the rows of folding chairs led to a stage barely a foot off the floor (the Second Fret folk club, Philadelphia, in September).

These were necessary steps, though, proof that the band were still going strong and building an audience, Sesnick reasoned, as he went searching for a new record deal for them. With the abject failure of *The Velvet Underground* came the end of their deal with Verve. Good riddance to them, Steve told Lou. Now he would go out and get them a proper recording contract with a record company that really knew what to do with a cutting-edge rock band like the Velvets. And this, to his lasting credit, Steve did, somehow talking the good people at Atlantic Records, over at Rockefeller Plaza in New York, into putting their weight behind the Velvet Underground, helping turn them into the next Cream or Led Zeppelin, both pioneers of the new breed of album-oriented acts the label was now having major coast-to-coast success with. Atlantic's only stipulation: that the album the band recorded for them had to be 'loaded with hits'. No more of that degenerate Warhol shtick, no more songs about shooting up and fucking sailors in the ass. Or as the popular music biz maxim went at the time: art for art's sake, hit records for fuck's sake! The kind of argument John Cale would have laughed out of the room. Or Andy would have just stared blankly at, like he had no idea what the straight guys were talking about. Or Nico would simply have lifted her dress and showed her ass to.

Lou, though, gamely complied. What else was he gonna do? The time for fucking around was over. He'd come so far down the road; it was too late to turn back now. And besides, what was there to go back to? His bridges had nearly all been burned. But when they were dropped by Verve, they also left behind enough material in the can for at least two albums, including such gems as 'I Can't Stand It', 'Stephanie Says' (apparently about Steve Sesnick: 'To Lou, everybody's gay', as Cale observed), 'Lisa Says', 'The Ocean', 'Andy's Chest' (inspired by the Solanas shooting), 'She's My Best Friend' and others that would later push their way back up through the undergrowth as Lou Reed solo tracks; while others like 'We're Gonna Have A Real Good Time Together', 'Foggy Notion', 'I'm Sticking With You', 'Ride Into The Sun' and 'Coney Island Steeplechase' would not resurface until years of bootlegs finally persuaded Verve to release them as two retrospective compilation albums in the mid-1980s, *VU* ('85) and *Another View* ('86).

But Lou just didn't care any more, that's what he told himself anyway. Which was partly true: John had been the real avant-gardist; Lou had always been the rock'n'roll adept. John barely saw the point of choruses; now Lou was free to write songs like 'Sweet Jane' that had such huge choruses they defied you not to sing along. Free to sit down and actually write a song called 'Rock And Roll'. Free at last to be a star, goddammit, motherfucker.

So it was that over the summer of 1969, when they weren't playing two-bit gigs to stoned hippies and their far-out old ladies in Cleveland, behind the scenes Lou Reed was writing the most commercial, self-consciously 'rock' songs of his career. It was almost like the Pickwick days again, except this time the musical masks he adopted would all be excellent facsimiles of Lou Reed – but with his fangs filed down and convincingly fake smiles painted on. The result – *Loaded*, named after Atlantic's line about making sure the album was *loaded* with hits – would become the most instantly likeable, undeniably catchy and, in time, most popular album the Velvet Underground would make. It was also the one that had the least input from any of its original founders. Lou may have written the songs but his heart was no longer breaking when he sang them, his brain no longer bubbling. He was having fun, playing at rock star, hanging out at gay afterhours bars in the Village with Billy one weekend, seeing Shelley the next. With the Stonewall riots in June – when 'overzealous' cops finally got their comeuppance after the regulars turned a bloody raid on the Village bar (long rumoured to be owned by the Mafia but well known for its day-to-day owners' kindness in offering sanctuary to the local gay and transgender community) into a full-scale riot which lasted, off and on, for several days – came the first evidence of what became known as gay activism, gay liberation and, eventually, new legislation decriminalising gay sex among consenting adults. It was a good time to be young, sexually polygamous and relatively free on the streets of downtown New York. When some of the marchers began carrying banners with slogans like 'WE'RE COMING OUT OF OUR CLOSETS', Lou chuckled wryly and took note: the line reappearing word for word three years later in the *Transformer* track 'Make Up'.

There were moments, though, when Lou wondered 'Just where I'm going', as he sang on 'Heroin', even as he determined to 'try for the kingdom, if I can...' Not least when he heard the second Nico solo album, *The Marble Index*, released that year and produced by Cale. It was like a ghost-of-Christmas-past midnight-hour journey to the place he might have gone had the Velvet Underground not been so quick to sell its soul. As Cale observed in his autobiography, *What's Welsh for Zen*, not having Lou there in the studio looking over his shoulder, trying to sex the songs up, 'allowed me carte blanche to bring in and use all this European stuff that I was happy with'. Nico burst into tears as he played her the finished tracks. 'Oh, it's so beautiful!' Her reaction to the new material being gathered together for *Loaded* – if she ever bothered to actually sit down and listen to it – is not known but can be easily deduced. Cale's less so. Indeed, in his autobiography he notes with an admirably straight face how 'everything had become more fragrant, the playing had become much gentler... Lou wanted to go into the pretty stuff.'

According to Maureen Tucker, Lou was so determined to get to that 'pretty place', by the end of 1969 he was even laying off the drugs, pointedly dropping 'Heroin' from the band's set list, and putting on weight again as a result. In its place had come yet more new songs that pointed to the future, including fractured early versions of 'Goodnight Ladies' (destined for *Transformer*), and 'Oh Jim' and 'Sad Song', both of which would four years later become cornerstone tracks on *Berlin*. More immediately came new songs, which would make it onto the next Velvets album, like 'Oh! Sweet Nothing', a hymnal salute to vacuity, which carried on the musically trancelike state of much of *The Velvet*

Underground but without the same sense of, albeit dimly lit, hope. And the similarly glacially paced 'New Age', ostensibly about a 'fat blonde actress' who is 'over the hill' but still 'looking for love': another reference to the emotionally stunted drag queens of the Warhol world, or a deeper look into the mirror by a 27-year-old man growing prematurely old under the weight of his own fears of failure?

On another new song written during this period, which would make it onto *Loaded*, 'I Found A Reason', which harks directly back to Lou's teenage obsession with doo-wop, the soft, cooing veneer belies the song's central message, which is uniformly dark: 'I do believe, if you don't like things you leave...'; similarly the other doo-wop-derived track which would eventually open the album, 'Who Loves The Sun', its glistening melody neatly masking its story of post-teen heartbreak. Even on throwaways like 'Lonesome Cowboy Bill' (yet another Warhol reference, this time to his 1968 'satire' *Lonesome Cowboys*) and 'Cool It Down' (which sounds like a musical parody of the kind of 'swinging cat' songs of the era like 'What's New Pussycat'), Lou finds it impossible to keep a straight face for long. As Sterling Morrison would confess to the New York writer Robert Greenfield, in an extraordinarily prophetic feature in the March 1970 edition of *Fusion*: 'Everybody's beaten. We've all lost, on every possible level.'

The same month the piece was published, Moe Tucker, who was five months pregnant, announced she would be taking a 'sabbatical' to have her baby. The band didn't even break stride, bringing in Doug Yule's younger brother, Billy, an accomplished but orthodox drummer whose presence would further undercut the unique sound of the Velvet Underground. When recording sessions for the album took place at Atlantic's New York studios at 1841 Broadway in April and May, Billy would drum on 'Lonesome Cowboy Bill' and 'Oh! Sweet Nothing', while an established session player, Tommy Castanero ('Cool It Down' and 'Head Held High'), and an English studio engineer, Adrian Barber ('Who Loves The Sun' and 'Sweet Jane'), were also drafted in to play drums. Moe would still be credited on the album sleeve but otherwise she had become another missing piece of the jigsaw, after Cale, Andy and Nico. (Although, in an unexpected footnote, John did agree to play on the initial recording of 'The Ocean', but the track was not included on the final album.) Diluting their musical palette further, Sterling now took a minimal interest in the music. He turned up, he played guitar, but he was far more involved now in the college studies that he'd lately resumed, in lieu of the smash hit success that Lou and Steve kept promising.

Ironically, just as Lou Reed had, on paper at least, assumed final control over the Velvet Underground, the band itself had never been so out of control, so unfocused; nor had they ever strayed so far from the original idea that they would not be like those other rock bands. Lou would persist in his pretence of knowing exactly what he was doing – and really honestly feeling very good about it – for a while longer but the signs of his own rapidly disintegrating faith in the band were most blatantly observed in the studio, where he encouraged Doug Yule to take a far greater role in proceedings. Not only did he now sing lead on four tracks – 'Who Loves The Sun', 'New Age', 'Lonesome Cowboy Bill' and 'Oh!

1967: the Velvet
Underground in a
rare shot outdoors,
celebrating their
Summer of Hate. Left
to right: John Cale,
Maureen Tucker,
Sterling Morrison, Lou
Reed. (Getty Images)

The Velvet Underground
at The Factory, Union
Square, New York,
1967. (Getty Images)

The Velvets at the Dom, East Village,
New York, 1966. Gerard Malanga brandishing
whip centre-stage. (Getty Images)

Andy (left) and Lou pose with one of Warhol's helium-
filled balloons entitled Silver Clouds, outside the Leo
Castelli gallery in New York, 1966. (Getty Images)

Classic Velvets pose, onstage with Nico
(in white) – at the Cinematheque in
1966. (Getty Images)

The Velvets – with Lou Reed *smiling* –
pretend to be The Monkees. Whose stupid
idea was that, Mr Record Company man?
From left, Moe and Lou (standing), John
and Sterling. (Getty Images)

Velvets MkIII: Lou, Sterling,
Moe and 'little brother'
Doug Yule, New York, 1970.
(Getty Images)

Andy and the extended 'family' at The Factory, 24 April 1969,
many of whom would be reborn in Lou Reed songs. (Getty Images)

The iconic Velvet Underground pose,
shot in 1966, but still instantly
recognisable today. (Getty Images)

Lou and Andy in the back room of
Max's Kansas City, after midnight, sometime
in 1968. Blonde in dress unknown
or whether she was a he. (Getty Images)

Onstage at the Bataclan club in Paris,
29 January 1972. The last time Reed, Cale
and Nico performed together. (Getty Images)

Sweet Nothing' – he also played guitar, bass and keyboards on all the tracks, as well as the drums on 'Rock And Roll', 'I Found A Reason' and 'Train Round The Bend'.

Indeed, Doug Yule was now taking such a large role in the band's music he would insist on co-writing credits with Lou, even going so far as to register the arrangements he had written for certain tracks with his own copyright. 'Little brother' Doug, the guy who'd been brought in to replace the thorn in Lou's side that Cale had become, was now threatening to take over the running of the whole ship. When Lou began to twig, he freaked out, copyrighting all the *Loaded* songs in his own name, rather than via the Velvets' joint publishing company, Virpi Music – including 'Who Loves The Sun', which he acknowledged as a joint composition with Doug. He also complained bitterly to Steve about the way things were going but Sesnick had his own pre-existing relationship with the Yule brothers and, what's more, felt the direction Doug was 'helping' Lou take the band in was the right one, certainly commercially, which was after all where his total focus lay. Steve, who had stood by Lou when everyone else was either bailing out or being pushed off the ledge, who had fed the band gigs at his own venue when no one else would let them through their doors, who had won them a major deal with one of the biggest old-money labels in the world when even niche-driven Verve had thrown in the towel, was rightfully looking for the pay-off. It seemed to him – and Atlantic – that Doug was helping Lou achieve it. What was the problem?

Doug, who understandably felt he was only asking for his fair share of credit – and money – for all the good work he was doing, saw it as any young musician would. Speaking years later, he recalled that on *Loaded* there was a real push to produce a hit single and a mentality of "which one of these [tracks] is a single, how does it sound when we cut it down to 3.5 minutes?" So that was a major topic for the group at that point. And I think that the [album] to a great extent shows a lot of that in that a lot of those songs were designed as singles and if you listen to them you can hear the derivation, like this is sort of a Phil Spector-ish kind of song, or this is that type of person song.'

By the time the Velvet Underground had begun what was to be their swan song engagement at Max's Kansas City – a projected ten-week stint in the impossibly hot summer of 1970 – Lou Reed was at his wits' end. Listening back in the studio to finished tracks like the towering 'Sweet Jane', destined to become one of his signature songs, with low-slung guitars and side-of-the-mouth vocal delivery, and 'Rock And Roll', another anthem to the younger Lou, whose 'life was saved by rock and roll', that again would become one of his landmark moments, he knew he had done something he never could have with John and Maureen and Nico and maybe even Sterling still vying for headspace in the studio, something so simple and amazing it restored his faith in his ability to go it alone, to trust his own instincts, to put it out there strictly on his own terms. Other tracks, though, like the awkward hey-mama raunch of 'Head Held High' – 'They said the answer was to become a dancer!' – would not have sounded out of place as the B-side of a Rolling Stones single. While the self-consciously woozy 'Train Round The Bend' could have been found on a Doors album – and Lou always hated Jim Morrison and The Doors.

But maybe he could have lived with all of that – produced by Atlantic's in-house engineer, Geoff Haslam, it had certainly the most lush, upbeat sound of any Velvets album – had he stuck around long enough to have seen the project through.

Instead, the summer shows at Max's would be Lou's last with the Velvet Underground. Some nights were better than others – as later evidenced on the 1972 album *Live At Max's Kansas City*. But with the Yule brothers bringing their more orthodox, disciplined style to the songs and the audience unsure whether Lou was sending it up with his absurdly over the top new Mick Jagger impersonation or actually just trying to *fit it* – like wow, Andy, this you gotta see! – these were largely grim affairs. The heady days when the backroom at Max's was a hive of salacious sex gossip, hyper-drive drug assignations and all-round circus-sewer fun were long gone. Lou didn't even bother checking out the scene anyway. When he wasn't onstage he was mostly seen holding up the bar alone, his face puffy beneath a butch new-boyfriend hairdo, throwing back the beers, one after the other, willing himself into a drunken oblivion.

Halfway through the run, Steve Sesnick decided he'd had enough. Taking Lou to task, he told him that he would continue to manage the Velvets, but his personal relationship with Lou was over. What this meant, in effect, it seemed to Lou, was that Steve was no longer interested in acting as his manager. He took it personally, though, typically. Speaking in 2003 of the ignominious way in which he felt he had been effectively fired from the Velvet Underground, Lou recalled the situation as 'just a terrible thing with the manager. Where the manager feels that he is more important than the artist, or is in competition with the artist. It's always a bad situation. You know, the manager has an apartment and the artist is sleeping on the floor by the fireplace like a sheepdog.'

Nevertheless, it was a devastating blow. Although he continued to act as the band's nominal front man, he felt like he'd been fired from his own band. Only ever inches away from full-blown paranoia, he now had every reason to believe that the others really were all against him. That he was, finally, alone. Lost. Wasted. Suddenly, the cocksure guy who had faced-down queen bitches like Andy Warhol, who had shown the door to musically intellectual superiors like John Cale, who had documented The Factory's best and worst days, becoming one with its tragic drag queens and leathered-up art freaks, living on speedballs and blowjobs, suddenly that guy had been reduced to what he really was: a vulnerable, oversensitive, small-town boy with overweening dreams of something... more.

When a few nights later the band arrived backstage at Max's they were astounded to find Lou standing there with his parents. They had come to take him home. A couple of days after that, on 23 August 1970, Lou Reed played his last gig as the leader of the Velvet Underground. He didn't tell the others, but knowing it would be his last show he insisted on bringing back into the set several lately discarded ballads, like 'Pale Blue Eyes' and 'Sunday Morning'. He even insisted on singing two of the songs he'd written for Nico to sing: 'I'll Be Your Mirror' and 'Femme Fatale'. His final song of the night, most poignantly, was Moe's 'After Hours'.

Of course, it was not the end of the Velvet Underground, whose fourth album, *Loaded*, would not be released for another three months. Having insinuated himself so deeply into the band's latter persona, and encouraged by Steve Sesnick, Doug Yule took over the fulltime reins of the band. Walter Powers, another boy from Boston, came in on bass but things were never the same without Lou. Moe Tucker returned some months later, but by the late summer of 1971 Sterling Morrison had finally had enough and quit for good, going on to qualify as a teacher. He was replaced by Doug's pal from The Glass Menagerie, the keyboardist Willie Alexander, who had played with Powers in an earlier Massachusetts band, The Lost. It was this line-up that was sent out on tour to promote *Loaded*, released in the US in November 1970, but not in the UK or mainland Europe until March the following year.

Lou looked on at this latest downturn in his fortunes with mixed feelings. On the one hand, it was pleasing, at last, to find one of his records was gaining some mainstream attention. Reviewing it in *Rolling Stone*, in December, fellow New Yorker and future Patti Smith guitarist Lenny Kaye described *Loaded* as one of his favourite albums of the year so far. Though also made the point that without Reed – till then their focal point as singer, songwriter and band leader – they would have a hard time finding any kind of replacement. Reading the review back home at his parents' place in Freeport, Lou could only grunt in agreement.

His own review of the finished album though was much less accommodating, He hated the mix, which had shorn several tracks of the elements he cherished most – the post-script bridge at the end of 'Sweet Jane'; the elongated end of 'New Age'; the newly inserted guitar break on 'Head Held

High'. Most heinously of all, complained Lou, 'The songs are out of order... they just leap about. They don't make sense thematically.' Well, maybe not to Lou. In fact, the arbitrary nature of the finished product is living testimony to the fact that, as Lou eventually had to admit, 'I just gave up on it. I wasn't there when it was done.'

The truth was nobody cared what Lou Reed thought about it any more. As far as Steve Sesnick and Doug Yule were concerned, it was now about promoting the album with the current line-up, and with Doug as its figurehead. When an up and coming singer from London named David Bowie visited New York for the first time in January 1971, and saw a poster for a gig at the Electric Circus (the new name for the Dom) by the Velvet Underground – a band he had become obsessed with since his then manager Kenneth Pitt had returned from a trip to New York in 1967 with a copy of their first album for him – he begged his record company liaison man, Ron Oberman to take him. Bowie had recently begun incorporating versions of, variously, 'I'm Waiting For The Man' and 'White Light/White Heat' into his own live set, and was blown away by his first taste of the band playing songs like 'Sweet Jane'. Pushing his way upstairs to the dressing room afterwards, determined to meet Lou Reed, he spent 10 minutes chatting to Doug Yule, assuming it was Lou, without anyone feeling the need to explain that Lou had actually left the band months before.

Subsuming the behind-closed-doors legend of Lou Reed within the overarching present-day reality of the newly configured group was considered a good marketing strategy back in 1971, in the days before the internet and multiple

TV channels, when word travelled at a snail's pace and names still in small print meant very little. And the Doug Yule-led Velvet Underground continued to tour off the back of *Loaded* through 1971, including no fewer than 23 concerts in Britain throughout October and November, interspersed with a handful of dates in Holland, Belgium and West Germany.

By now the cult of the Velvet Underground – not of Lou Reed – had spread to the London-based music press, who were becoming the gatekeepers for all music that lay beyond the purview of the islands' only national radio station playing pop music. Never having had the chance to see the Velvet Underground perform live before, the press considered the recent loss of Lou Reed a blow but not necessarily an insurmountable one. Interviewed in the *NME*, Doug Yule tried to explain it away as some sort of natural evolution: it had once been more Lou Reed's group, that was true. But now it was more his group. Simple, dimples. Catching the same show at Kingston Polytechnic, on 9 October, where, as *NME* writer Tony Stewart concluded: 'Gone is the gimmicky lights show ... and Warhol's influence had obviously waned.'

My own teenage memory of that event is of none of my circle of friends – including older, college-age brothers and girlfriends – knowing for sure whether it was Lou Reed on stage or not. There were certainly no clues offered on the tickets or posters or any of the adverts we'd seen in the music papers. None of us had a clear idea of what he looked like, outside the blurry images on VU sleeves, most of which captured him in sunglasses and nondescript sweaters. We were still arguing about it weeks and months afterwards. One thing we did agree on: it had been a great show. But what did we know, most of us, including me, still living at home with our parents?

What we definitely could not have imagined was that at home with Mum and Dad was exactly where Lou Reed was living now too. Not only that but he was actually working nine to five each day at his father's tax consultancy firm, in Long Island City, where Sidney had procured him a nice steady job as a typist. As Lou would later put it, apparently without irony: 'My mother always told me in high school: "You should take up typing. It gives you something to fall back on." She was right.'

Around the same time, Lou began a relationship with the new love of his life, a pretty young blonde named Bettye Kronstad. Like Lou, Bettye lived on Long Island with her middle-class Jewish parents. Despite her regular visits to the beauty salon, her strings of pearls and pretty summer dresses, Bettye, like Lou, dreamed of a world outside those conservative restraints, attending acting classes where she went by the stage name of Krista – a name that sounded the same as Nico's actual one, an odd coincidence that Lou saw as entirely in keeping with all the other so-called chance meetings in his life so far. It wasn't Nico's high-priced brand of love Lou sought in Bettye though but the same kind of familial fire that had drawn him to Shelly Albin, with whom Bettye shared the same boyish figure, charitable emotions and warm sexy smile.

Lou may have retreated from the seedy New York milieu that had made him (almost) famous but he was still a young man who dealt in desperate extremes. If he was to abandon his life as a rock'n'roller, living on the road and sleeping on the floors of others, for a new, more centred life of cosy routine, salaried job and a good, clean comfortable home among the manicured gardens of suburbia, he was going to do it to the maximum. The addition of an unflinchingly heterosexual relationship with a straight-up gal like Bettye was seen as the next big step towards living out that new fantasy in full.

Writing in the hip music and culture magazine *Fusion*, in earnest preface to a series of love poems he published in its pages, in Bettye's honour, Lou declared: 'Bettye is not hip at all, and I want to keep her that way. I believe in pretty princesses.' In his poem, simply titled 'Bettye', he wrote. 'I think I am in love / I seem to have the symptoms / (ignore past failures in human relations / I think of Bettye all the time)...'

He began to write reams of poetry, much of it devoted to Bettye, a great deal of it clearly more concerned with his own malaise – much of which *Fusion* was happy to publish. Seeing himself less as a musician, his guitars left for now to gather dust in his parents' spacious garage, and more as a fulltime wordsmith, Lou still mulled endlessly over his own fate, much as he had done at Syracuse when he looked to Delmore Schwartz for his inspiration, but now with the bruised hindsight and clipped vision of a man who had been through the treadmill, only to emerge more unsure than ever.

In his poem titled 'Waste' he wrote of a wasted education, a mind scrambled by drugs and a life of newfound boredom. Clearly his new life at home with Sidney and Toby, or snuggled up warm on the bed with Bettye, was something even he found hard to believe sometimes. In his poem 'He Thought Of Love In The Lazy Darkness', a tale of a dark soul contemplating a saintly lover, he confesses to indecision 'dissolving you like a mint' or 'crushing you like a ladybug'. It appeared as though his career as a budding poet might actually come to something more when, in March 1971, he was invited to give a reading at a Poetry Project being staged at St Mark's Church in Manhattan. In front of an audience that included, to his initial horror, Allen Ginsberg and several well-known members of the Warhol set, he began with some Velvet Underground lyrics before moving on to his love poems to Bettye, before concluding with some more recent, more gay-themed poems. Receiving a standing ovation at the end, he boldly announced that he would not be returning to sing rock'n'roll, but would from now on be dedicating his life to writing poetry – adding that if he did ever go back to being in a band Delmore Schwartz's ghost would probably come back to haunt him.

And so things might have continued – at least for a while longer – had not Lou Reed's career as a songwriter, considered moribund since walking off the stage at Max's nine months before, begun to twitch slowly back into life, in the spring of 1971. Receiving an offer to write the 'book' – that is, the music and lyrics – for a prospective Broadway musical based on Nelson Algren's classic 1956 underground novel *A Walk On The Wild Side*. According to its author, the book 'asks why lost people sometimes develop into greater human beings than those who have never been lost in their whole lives'. In 1962, the novel had been turned into the movie, *Walk On The Wild Side*, starring Laurence Harvey and Jane Fonda, with a screenplay written by another off-the-radar novelist – and Reed favourite – named John Fante. Finding it literary enough to flatter him, musical enough without requiring him to work a rock band again, Lou leapt at the chance.

Unfortunately, as most often happens with such ideas, the pitch never got off the ground and Lou was left thwarted, yet with the framework of an idea for a song called 'Walk On The Wild Side' – no longer directly related to the Algren novel, but about several of the real-life personalities he had encountered in his Factory days. No longer told from the bitchy eye of the hurricane, as all his previous songs about the Warhol scene had been, but from his new, fresh perspective, as someone who had – apparently – left that all behind but still retained enormous empathy for the basic, always overlooked humanity of the central characters.

When another friend from New York, Danny Fields, invited Lou and Bettye over for dinner with his friends Richard Robinson and his wife Lisa, one evening in May 1971, Lou told them the story and played them the earliest, still sketchy version of the song. Intrigued, Richard and Lisa egged Lou on to play anything else he'd been working on lately. There wasn't a great deal so instead he simply sang some of the many songs that had been abandoned or lost along the way when the deal with Verve went south and the bigwigs at Atlantic took over the picking and choosing; among them such still - hidden gems as 'The Ocean', 'Walk It And Talk It' and 'Love Makes You Feel Ten Foot Tall'.

Richard and Lisa – used to spending their evenings hanging out with a range of New York's finest underground poet-musicians like Patti Smith, Jim Carroll and Richard Hell – were so bowled over they felt moved to act. Lisa was then writing for *Creem* and she became the first person to start talking about Lou Reed and his new music to other writers such as Hennery Edwards, who wrote for the *New York Times*, and Richard Meltzer, a turned-on Yale graduate then writing for *Crawdaddy* but soon to become a leading voice for *Rolling Stone*, *Creem* and the *Village Voice*.

Richard was then working as a house-producer at RCA Records, a giant label whose reputation in the contemporary music field rested on its ownership of all Elvis Presley's recordings. Lately, though, it had begun to wake up to the same album-oriented artist that its more forward-thinking competitors like Atlantic and Warner Bros had, releasing the first John Denver album in 1969 and, most recently, securing the signature of a certain David Bowie, whose American manager, Tony De Fries, had sold them to RCA's youngest, sharpest A&R executive, Dennis Katz, as the next big star of the 1970s.

It would not be easy, Richard Robinson told Lou Reed, that summer of 1971, but if Richard could figure it out, how would Lou like to come and make an album or two with RCA? This poetry thing was great, man, you know, but, hey, do you know how much dough the company just paid out for this Bowie cat? And he's doing the same kind of thing you've been doing for years?

Whaddayasay, Lou? You in?

5
Breakup To Makeup

The latter half of 1971 was all about getting ready to launch Lou Reed on an unsuspecting and, frankly, disinterested world. The intrepid Richard and Lisa Robinson aside, who else actually gave a shit about a broken-down old homo from Warhol's better days, before Valerie came in and spoiled the party with her boom-boom-boom?

One man: David Bowie. Yes, Lou Reed, who'd relied on father-figure mentors going back to Delmore Schwartz and carrying on through John Cale, Andy Warhol, Steve Sesnick and, right now while it suited him, Richard Robinson, who would help get him signed to RCA and produce his first solo album, was about to be saved yet again by someone who didn't just dig him for his barbed tongue or indoor shades but who actually recognised his talent. In fact, without the intervention of David Bowie, it seems highly unlikely now that Lou Reed would ever have had a career, certainly not beyond the risk-averse two-album deal he signed with Dennis Katz at RCA in the late summer of 1971.

The two had finally met for real in September that year, when Bowie was flown into New York to great fanfare, in order to celebrate his signing to RCA. Dennis Katz, via Richard and Lisa Robinson, brokered the meeting, organising a big party at the Ginger Man, around the corner from Madison Avenue. Lou turned up with Bettye and David showed up with his American wife, Angie. Tony Zanetta, who was currently playing the role of Andy in Warhol's off-Broadway show *Pork*, was expected to make the introductions. Although he'd never actually met Lou before, Tony had bonded with David and Angie during the show's recent run in London, and nervously affected introductions. Thankfully Lisa Robinson, a skilled socialite in New York rock circles, kept the whole shebang going, covering any awkward pauses with trilling tra-la-la gossip. She needn't have worried. Lou didn't shut up, his insecurities raging as he confronted the coming English star he'd been told had been featuring Velvet Underground songs in his set, and who he was now connected directly to through their shared relationship with RCA and, specifically, its vice-president of A&R, Dennis Katz.

Bowie for his part remained relatively quiet, overwhelmed by the force of the always heavily loaded New York conversation, not sure who was putting who on, who was being put down, or what any of this might actually have to do with him. While Angie Bowie, of course, could match Lisa or Lou or indeed anyone else for fast-track trash talk, NY-style, honey. Bettye, meanwhile, sat quietly, obediently, in her pants suit, looking like 'an airline stewardess' in one onlooker's bitchy but memorable phrase. Lou, for his part, hardly looked like the hip young former Factory fop Bowie had been expecting.

While David was going through his 'Lauren Bacall phase', his blonde hair long and swept over one shoulder, his eyelashes fluttering under the weight of heavy blue shadow, Lou had turned up looking like the guy who came to fix the plumbing; dressed down in head-to-toe denim, paunchy, his hair cut almost army short. The two left a lasting impression on each other, both agreeing to talk 'seriously' some other time, when they weren't being watched quite so closely and by so many people at once. It would be sooner than Lou thought. As Bowie told reporters upon his return to London: 'Lou has been a powerful influence on a host of contemporary performers – myself included.'

But there the association ended – at least for now. Lou, meanwhile, had plans to make. Number one was finding a new manager, after Danny Fields turned him down, rightly predicting just how high maintenance Lou as a client would be. Indeed, Lou's all-hours phone habit was so bad at the time that the Robinsons had a special private number they made those that had it swear they wouldn't pass on to Lou, who was phoning on the Robinsons' number he did have dozens of a times a day (and night). He finally settled on Fred Heller, then managing jazz-rock fusion stars Blood, Sweat & Tears, who were riding hot and heavy on the American charts with two No. 1 albums, and whose guitarist, Steve, was Dennis Katz's younger brother (and whose brilliant drummer, Bobby Colomby, had just played on John Cale's innovative album collaboration with Terry Riley, *Church Of Anthrax*, released the same year).

Fred would always insist on calling him Lewis, but he knew his shit and Lou was impressed as between them Fred and Dennis arranged for Lou and Bettye to fly to London – along with Richard Robinson, who would produce, and Lisa, who would 'coordinate' – to record his first solo album, at Morgan Studios, in January 1972; the same venue where recent smash hits had been fashioned by Led Zeppelin, Rod Stewart, Paul McCartney, Jethro Tull, Cat Stevens and dozens of others.

London made sense for a number of other reasons too: it got Lou out of New York, where familiarity had long since bred the contempt of his contemporaries; it also gave him room to breathe, away from the intruding presence of the RCA higher-ups not as attuned to the new emerging rock scene as Dennis Katz, and who were still nervous about investing in what others saw as an already four-time loser. And it put Lou into a city where his music with the Velvet Underground was much more venerated than in its home town. Bowie's patronage had helped see to that, as he now regularly name-checked Lou in interviews, going so far as to record a track, the glorious 'Queen Bitch', on his own just-released album, *Hunky Dory*, which he not only 'borrowed' the riff from 'Sweet Jane' for but was cheeky enough to admit as much in the sleeve notes, giving thanks for some 'VU white light'. It was also true that a small but passionate band of Velvet Underground followers had flowered in London since the days when Brian Epstein turned John Lennon on to the first VU album in 1967; the Beatles' manager had been talking of bringing the band to London, possibly even managing them, just before his suicide the same year. Ironically, the British tour at the end of 1971 by the Doug Yule-led VU line-up had also kicked up a lot of renewed interest in his immediate past and suddenly whenever Lou Reed's name was fleetingly mentioned in the British music press it came prefaced with the appellation 'legendary'.

RCA in London had also, at the behest of Dennis Katz, marshalled what was then considered to be a crack team of session men to play on the album, which would be simply titled *Lou Reed*. So that when Lou turned up for his first session at Morgan, in north London, waiting for him were players including most famously the keyboardist Rick Wakeman, then of Yes, but who had also just done the business on Bowie's *Hunky Dory*; the guitarists Steve Howe, also of Yes, and Caleb Quaye, then of Elton John's studio band; the drummer Clem Cattini, veteran of hundreds of sessions for everyone from The Tornados and Cliff Richard and the Shadows, to the Bee Gees and Joe Cocker, and who had passed on the opportunity of joining Led Zeppelin, who then switched their attention to John Bonham.

Staying with Bettye in a suite at the plush Inn On The Corner, *the* hotel for visiting American rock stars to be seen at in London in the early 1970s, where he revelled for the first time in the mysteries and privileges of being waited on night and day as if he were a really famous American rock star too, walking around exploring London on his days off, Richard on one arm and Bettye on the other, introducing them oh so amusingly to everyone they met as 'my boyfriend and my girlfriend', the only place where Lou wasn't completely comfortable and confident, disastrously and unexpectedly so, was the recording studio.

Intimidated by the sheer array of musical talent before him – it was one thing to have to live up to the expectations of avant-gardists like Cale and Warhol, quite another to hold your own as a straight singer in the company of such seasoned professional musicians as Rick Wakeman and Steve Howe – Lou abdicated responsibility for directing the sessions entirely to Richard. The problem was Robinson – who'd just done such a great job of capturing the live excitement of the Flamin' Groovies on their cult hit, *Teenage Head* – never quite caught the sound everyone who knew the Velvet Underground was hoping for from a Lou Reed solo album. Then, Lou was so abashed at the prospect of plugging in and playing his guitar in such exalted company, he took the previously unheard of decision to absent himself completely from the playing side, the better to concentrate on his singing, he said, which he was also clearly struggling with. Suddenly insecure about the low-rider gangster-speak of his usual vocal style on his albums with the Velvets, under pressure from within to try and comply with what he assumed would be the high expectations of his studio band, at the very moment he should have had things positioned exactly how he wanted them, Lou was so unsure he utterly lost his voice, figuratively.

It didn't help that almost every track lined up to be recorded had originally been written for and moulded by the Velvet Underground – whose music, he soon discovered to his further discomfiture, none of the assembled musos were remotely familiar with. Thus what onstage with the Velvet Underground two years before had sounded like promisingly vintage Lou Reed vignettes, such as the album opener, 'I Can't Stand It' – over six minutes long in its original more louche incarnation, here clipped to a taught 2.35 – now became a slicked-back lightweight rocker. Same deal with 'Ocean', which closes the album. What had become one of the great lost moments of the Velvet Underground, over ten minutes long, as it was first played live throughout 1969, sweeping, dark, majestic in its gathering gloom, now on *Lou Reed* would become Dracula-by-numbers. The band had come the closest they could to reproducing the original atmosphere with the guitars, but the production is lessened rather than enhanced by the addition of crashing gongs and cymbals, Wakeman's neo-classical running-down-the-corridor-in-fear piano and, worst of all, Reed's cringe-inducing vocal performance, overreaching horribly as he tries to find the extra gravitas the original had had dripping from its dog-chewed fingertips.

Between times we get the same variations on a theme: a handful of Velvet Underground-era classics-in-the-making – the musicianly 'Walk And Talk It' (previously the grimy 'Walk And Talk'); the get-up-and-go 'Ride In The Sun', with the admittedly joyful guitar interplay of Howe and Quaye (formerly the gorgeously spaced-out VU elegy); 'Lisa Says', Lou leaning forward into the mike as the band pick out some tasteful country blues behind him, compared to the snaking, regretful 1969 original – served up as the dainty dish of a songwriter of the order of a James Taylor or an Elton John. In retrospect it's perfectly understandable why they did it. The early 1970s was the golden era of the tortured but musically gifted singer-songwriter. Carole King – another artist with a past she was now trying to live down, although in King's case, not as a drug fiend but as a clean-cut production-line writer of pop hits at New York's famous Brill Building

– had a No. 1 hit in the US in 1971 with her introspective masterpiece *Tapestry*; James Taylor had sold three million copies of his debut solo album, *Sweet Baby James*. Even as they were recording Lou Reed, Neil Young was hitting No. 1 in Britain and America with *Harvest*. Even an avowed populist like Rod Stewart, whose goodtime band the Faces failed dismally to impact on the charts, now found enormous commercial success with a solo album, *Every Picture Tells A Story*, that reintroduced him to the wider audience as a 'meaningful' singer-songwriter. Hadn't Bowie also just done his own singer-songwriter trip with *Hunky Dory*?

Most unctuous of all are the 'new' songs that came after Lou had walked out of Max's that night: 'Going Down', 'I Love You' and 'Berlin'; all perfectly serviceable love songs, given that joss stick and hessian musical ambience which was now considered the tasteful norm, the former brace witheringly sanitised versions of their stark 1970 demos, the latter containing only a passingly redeemable opening verse and piano part that would, in time, find new life in death on the far greater album of the same name.

The only track that really made it on *Lou Reed* was 'Wild Child'. Another VU leftover, but which had never got any further than a rough acoustic cassette recording, while still suffering from the English politeness of the backing, the lyrics are so good – and the singing, for once, more like the confident Lou of old – it would have sounded right at home on *Loaded*, sitting next to such similarly conversational but otherwise straightforward nouveau rock classics as 'Sweet Jane' and 'Rock And Roll'. It even squeezed in a line for Bettye: 'I was talking to Bettye about her auditions, how they made her ill...' Indeed, RCA missed a trick when it chose as the first single from the album the relatively lack-lustre 'I Can't Stand It', then wondered why everyone was so underwhelmed.

Lou was bitterly disappointed. Despite his lifelong protes-tations about not caring about having hit singles, he would have liked nothing better just then than to shove it down the throat of everyone in New York who had ever bad-mouthed him by having a big fat chart hit. When, during the recording of *Lou Reed* in London, Richard Robinson burst through the door one day to tell him that Mitch Ryder's version of 'Rock And Roll' – a much hairier, more leery and macho version than the original on *Loaded* – had just jumped into the *Billboard* Hot 100 at No. 95, Lou was thrilled.

'Isn't that just great!' Lou remarked to the writer Steve Turner, who was interviewing him for a piece in the British muso mag *Beat Instrumental*. 'I've finally made the Hot 100! I'm 95, God help us!' Then added: 'I'd love to have a Number One. That'd be great, wouldn't it?'

Hit singles or not, Lou quickly regained his composure. Interviewed at the time of the album's release, in April 1972, by Richard Williams of the *Melody Maker*, he maintained that 'As far as I'm concerned it's the album we need most of all right now, the one which takes us above and beyond all the [Warhol] superstar crap and back into music.'

That wasn't the way Dennis Katz at RCA felt about it though when Lou got back to New York and played him the tapes. The rest of the RCA executive team were so appalled they announced they would release the album, if only to try and claw back some of the significant sums they had already spent on it, but that they were cancelling the second album and dropping Reed from the label. But Katz fought back, taking over the day-to-day management of Lou himself personally, and booking dates for what would be his first solo tour.

Freaked out by Dennis's obvious disappointment, unsure how to go about putting a band together to back him on his tour, Lou retreated to the tiny new Upper East Side apartment he and Bettye had moved into and began drinking even more heavily. Bettye bore most of the brunt of his frustration, as he took to 'teasing' her about his previous life in New York, how he missed sucking cock. He had also taken to hitting her. As another Warhol acolyte, the writer Glenn O'Brien, later recalled of that time to Victor Bockris: 'I remember her always having a black eye.'

When Lou hired a Village bar band called The Tots as his new backing group, perhaps Dennis Katz thought it was a shrewd move on the singer's part to try and distance himself from the slick but soulless music of *Lou Reed*, in an attempt to rekindle some of the street-level gutter vine of the original Velvets. In fact, Lou was simply trying to find a band that would do what they were told and wouldn't try and outshine him musically. In guitarists Vinny Laporta and Eddie Reynolds, bassist Bobby Resigno and drummer Scottie Clark he found exactly that. They didn't know the Velvets' catalogue, only knew of Lou's story what he chose to tell them, but were a tight little band who learned quick and were happy to find themselves working with a genuine recording artist with a deal and money behind him. Lou was just happy he didn't have to answer to anyone.

Those first shows were freakish though. As if to conceal his sheer terror at going out on tour as a solo artist for the first time, Lou overcompensated by for the first time dressing the way he thought a rock star would. In the summer of 1972, with Bowie and glam rock beginning its rapid ascendancy, Lou replaced the denims with a leather jacket and trousers that he'd bought especially from Hernando's on Christopher Street – the same place Andy used to shop for his leathers. His dark bushy hair was growing out again now too, providing a sort of giant halo of curls, like flies, framing a face whose chubby cheeks he now masked in white pancake and heavy black eyeliner. A terrible look made worse by the fact he was still not playing guitar, coming on like an overweight fag Jim Morrison, but without the beard and with none of the charisma.

The disappointment was felt in earnest when *Lou Reed* was released in May. Despite picking up good reviews in *Fusion*, where Lou, of course, was still a contributor (though with the caveat that the band were 'strictly back-up'), and *Phonograph Record* (which also added tellingly: 'How successful is an album that keeps you imagining what it would sound like with the rest of the guy's former group?'), the heavy hitters like Robert Christgau in the *Village Voice* (who grudgingly gave it a B+, commenting: 'He sounds not just "decadent" but jaded, fagged out') and Lester Bang in *Creem* ('Edith Piaf, he ain't') did not bother to hide their bafflement and disappointment. When the album sold fewer than 10,000 copies in its first couple of weeks, it was official: *Lou Reed* was a lame duck.

When within weeks, a 'new' Velvet Underground album – *Live At Max's Kansas City* – was released, the comparisons between Lou Reed the straight man solo artist and Lou Reed the once maverick leader of the most significant cult band in the world were all too easy to make. Looking back three decades later, Lou was wont to make light of the situation, going so far as to claim that he had actually masterminded the inopportune release of *Live At Max's* himself. 'A friend of mine got me out of Atlantic Records by giving them a cassette that was recorded at Max's Kansas City which was released as a mono record called *The Velvet Underground Live At Max's* [sic] and that got me out. And then they got me signed to RCA as a solo. And then at that time the records in the UK just had a better sound to them. Better engineers, better studios, you know, for non-r'n'b stuff. So that was the reason to come over here.'

In fact, Brigid Polk had recorded the show on her tiny cassette recorder on the very night, two years before, that Lou had played his last set with the band. Far from being some chess move made by Lou to free him from his deal with Atlantic, he had long since left the band by the time Steve Sesnick found out about Brigid's tape and offered her a modest sum to release it to him, and then offered it to Atlantic, in lieu of a final VU album, while he was actually busy making a new deal for the Yule-led line-up with Atlantic rivals Polydor. Whatever the machinations behind the scenes that resulted in *Live At Max's*, coming as it did hard on the heels of the antiseptic *Lou Reed*, it appeared as damning testament to the career path the singer now found himself mincing down. A sad indictment of a once great talent gone tragically to waste. Inevitably, it picked up better reviews too. When it also started to outsell *Lou Reed*, Lou was beside himself with rage and self-pity, and Bettye's days just got worse.

Enter his knight in shiny sequins: David Bowie. Released on RCA in June 1972, Bowie's new album, *The Rise And Fall Of Ziggy Stardust And The Spiders From Mars*, had finally turned the erstwhile Davey Jones into a global superstar. A massive critical and commercial success in Britain, although it would not cross the threshold into the US Top 30, such was the acclaim it was afforded by the critical establishment, that Bowie was now able to headline his own major tours of America, propped up by the extravagant budgets RCA were prepared to lavish on him. Now when he returned to New York that summer he stayed at the Sherry Netherland, a 38-floor luxury apartment hotel on Fifth Avenue. When, again, he inquired after Lou Reed, he was dismayed to learn of the onerous false start he had made with his own RCA career. With Bowie then apparently on a mission to rescue the careers of other fallen idols of his like Mott The Hoople – whose Bowie-penned and produced single, 'All The Young Dudes', had been a huge hit in Britain and was now racing up the US Top 40 – and Iggy Pop, whose band the Stooges – a cult like the Velvets, unknown outside Detroit until Bowie began eulogising them to the UK music press – he also now planned to resuscitate by producing, when he floated the idea of perhaps producing an album for Lou Reed as well, Dennis Katz moved fast.

Only snag: Bowie's touring schedule was now being mapped out for the rest of 1972. If he were going to work with Lou in the studio it would have to be *now*. Lou didn't need to be told twice. Neither did Katz, a literary man who felt Lou's work had been badly served by the musicianship and production on *Lou Reed*. To have the opportunity of putting Lou back in the studio with another, clearly much more simpatico producer, but also an artist who was 'hot as a pistol' right then, was almost too good to be true.

It wasn't just what Bowie might bring to his work in the studio that convinced Reed and his new manager to go ahead. It was what else such a close association with the indefatigable English singer would entail: entrée into the fashionable new world of 1970s glitter rock. Just as Andy Warhol had been Lou's ticket to the bleeding edge of 1960s pop culture, Lou hitched his wagon now to the fastest rising new 'superstar' of the 1970s – another iconoclast in the making who knew how to work that rich but still largely unexplored seam where music, art, fashion, omni-sexuality, fast drugs, film and TV could collide before splintering off into other ever more far-out forms of truth and expression, and with that, trailing in its wake like obedient puppy dogs on diamond-encrusted leads, money and fame and no going home again ever.

Sessions at London's Trident Studios, where Bowie had made both *Hunky Dory* and *Ziggy Stardust*, were hastily booked for late July, early August. Ken Scott, the gifted studio veteran who had assisted Bowie on the recordings of both those lustrous albums, was also engaged by Bowie for the Lou Reed sessions. Bowie also offered Lou the chance to fly to London early, in order to make a guest appearance at his big headline show at the Royal Festival Hall, on 8 July – a benefit concert organised by Friends Of The Earth in aid of Save The Whale.

Bowie had performed on the nation's most – watched music TV programme, *Top Of The Pops*, two days before, performing his *Ziggy* hit 'Starman', and the audience was a freakish mix of committed hippies and teenage glitter kids. When the compere, the Radio One DJ Kenny Everett, introduced Bowie to the stage as 'the next biggest thing to God', the crowd went suitably wild, stamping and cheering. In his spiky red hair and tight white *Clockwork Orange* suit, Bowie was at the height of his newfound fame, surfing that moment which comes only once in the lifetime of a star of that magnitude, where everything they touch turns to gold. When, for the encores, he announced he would like to introduce 'a very special friend' to the stage and Lou Reed walked out, still in the same ghoulish all black outfit and thick white pancake make-up, the truth is very few of those present knew or cared who this was, only that their beloved darling David seemed to like him so they would too. It was the impact Lou's appearance at such a pivotal Bowie show had on the music press that really counted, though. The three Velvet Underground songs Bowie brought Reed on to perform – 'I'm Waiting For The Man', 'White Light/White Heat' and 'Sweet Jane' – acted as the surest form of blessing from on high imaginable in that still innocent London summer. Suddenly, it didn't matter whether you'd heard of Lou Reed or his old band or not, didn't even matter if you liked what you heard or not, the fact that David Bowie was clearly so involved with him made Lou Reed the most fashionable American rock star in the world, briefly. At least, as far as papers like the *NME* and the *Melody Maker* were concerned. Which is all that mattered to Lou at that point anyway.

When Bowie held a press reception at the Dorchester Hotel in Mayfair, just days before going into Trident to begin the album that would become *Transformer*, he made sure Lou was also in attendance. 'Three changes of dress and a kiss from Lou Reed. The waiters were horrified,' began the report from the legendary Charles Shaar Murray, in the *NME*. 'Lou Reed is talking quietly to David,' the story went on in suitably hushed tones. 'He's wearing shades and maroon fingernails. Periodically, horrified waiters enter to deliver yet more Scotch and wine and sandwiches.'

Then, speaking directly to Bowie, Murray pinned him down about his apparent infatuation with Reed, suggesting that 'Lou Reed was to you as Chuck Berry was to the Stones?'

'Yes, very much so,' Bowie replied. 'That's a very good analogy, and I agree with it entirely. In fact, I've said the same myself on numerous occasions.'

Later on in the interview Bowie played Murray a tape of the yet to be released Mott The Hoople album, which opened with a version of 'Sweet Jane', suggested to them by Bowie. 'Fabulous,' said Bowie, 'really good...'

Murray agreed, proclaiming it 'the best I've ever heard' Mott. Bowie then talked briefly about the new record he was about to make with Lou. Suggesting that, while in VU tracks like 'Waiting For The Man', 'Lou captured, for me better than anyone else, the feeling of New York, that particular area of New York that he was living in and those times', the new material he was writing then would 'surprise a lot of people as well. It's miles different from anything he's ever done before.'

While Murray was taking that titbit in, Bowie turned to

another journalist and proclaimed: 'Any society that allows people like Lou and me to become rampant is pretty well lost.'

'He's very smart and very, very talented and I met him in New York and thought this guy would be a really fun guy to work with,' Lou would later recall of those days with Bowie. 'David just understood [Lou],' said Ken Scott. 'Which no one else did, in the state he was in.' Yet it was Bowie's right-hand man, onstage and in the studio, Mick Ronson, that Lou would find himself working with most closely during the coming weeks at Trident.

A talented guitarist, pianist, producer, singer and arranger, 'Ronno' it was who more than anyone was able to coax Lou into giving some of the best recorded performances of his career. 'Mick Ronson's arrangements were killer,' Lou recalled. He added with a smile: 'The thing about Ronno was that I could never understand a word that he said, it's like, he's from Hull. You had to ask him eight times to say something. And he was like "Ouzibuzziwoozy"... I mean, sweet guy, but incomprehensible. Completely. But listen to that arrangement of "Perfect Day". I mean that's Ronson. But David is no slouch, I mean, we were rehearsing for our little show and we're doing "Satellite Of Love" and we were doing the real background part at the end, and the guys were really admiring David and going, "Holy shit, what a part that is!" He outdid himself.'

It was Bowie though whose job it would be to talk Lou down from whatever emotional rollercoaster he happened to be riding that day. Still hugely insecure about exactly what his role should be now he was a bona fide solo artist, Lou had also begun self-medicating again, on booze, on pills – both downers like Mandrax and amphetamines like the blues and black bombers then common on the London scene – anything he could get his hands on to help him sleepwalk through the sessions. Ronson would later recall how 'laid-back' Lou was in the studio. How he'd sit down and start playing his guitar, seemingly oblivious to the fact it was 'way out of tune'. Ronson would wander over and tune it up for him while he still held it in his lap. 'He'd just look at me like he didn't really care if it was in tune or out of tune.' Dai Davies, who was then Bowie's personal press advisor, and was present at some of the Trident sessions, would describe Reed to the writer Paul Trynka as 'Extremely messed up. Like a parody of a drug fiend.'

Nevertheless, work proceeded extremely quickly. Bowie liked to work at lightning speed anyway, but with the added pressure of his own rapidly escalating solo career, and the pressures of also helping to oversee the rebirth of both Mott The Hoople and Iggy Pop, there was no time to lose. Three of the backing tracks were completed in one day, with both Ronson and Bowie going in and playing the parts themselves that Lou would be taking too long to deliberate over, as well as singing a variety of backing vocals and even, in David's case, adding a lush and inspiring harmony vocal arrangement to 'Satellite Of Love' which turned it from another old Velvets leftover into one of the stand-out tracks on an album brimming with highlights. It was ostensibly about someone so insane with jealousy over a recalcitrant love they become their stalker, but Bowie's full-throated backing vocals also inadvertently tapped into Lou's love of old doo-wop records. 'The really great thing is the high note at the end,' Reed recalled years later in the superb TV documentary about the making of *Transformer* in the *Classic Albums* series. 'That was the exclamation mark. Very few people could do that. Really pure and beautiful...'

The whole album was a hit from start to finish. In an age when 'serious' rock artists, including Bowie, were fond of describing their latest albums as 'concepts', Reed would make no such claim for *Transformer*, yet it was one of the most fully realised concept albums of the era. From the singeing opener, 'Vicious', which Lou explained had – yet again – been inspired by something Andy Warhol once said, when he suggested Lou write a song called 'Vicious' (Lou: 'I said, "'Vicious' like what?" He said, "Oh, I don't know. Like 'Vicious' hit me with a flower"'), to the outrageously camp yet strangely poignant album closer, 'Goodnight Ladies' (its heaving tuba, whistling clarinet brass band hacking inspired by several viewings of the Broadway musical director Bob Fosse's 1972 film *Cabaret*, starring Liza Minnelli and set in the Berlin of the Weimar Republic), *Transformer* was the album, for good or ill, that came to define everyone's idea of Lou Reed *without* the Velvet Underground. Including, ultimately, that of Reed himself, whether dragging his music and persona as far away from it as possible – or at least *trying* to – or revelling in its refracted glory, at first living it, being it, then sending it up, putting it down, even reusing the iconic cover image a decade later on *The Blue Mask*, the album that went a long way – though not quite far enough – to finally burying the old junkie-transsexual, journalist-slayer image *Transformer* left him shrouded in.

The new songs were simply so good. The most famous – 'Walk On The Wild Side' and 'Perfect Day' – were as good as anything he would ever write. Both relied for their universal appeal on the superb production touches of both Bowie and Ronson. On the latter, Ronno both played the so-tender piano parts and arranged the orchestral strings that lift the song out of the maudlin emotional dustbowl it could have been, and into something utterly transcendent and, as Reed put it, 'pure'. Indeed, with its tinkling fairy-tale melody and dark afterhours lyrics, a wonderful juxtaposition that reaches its apotheosis on the line, 'I thought I was someone else, someone good', 'Perfect Day' could be read on a number of levels. No more so than when, 25 years later, it would go to No. 1 in the UK, as the basis for a children's charity single. But that wasn't what Lou was singing about on the original track at all. 'It's not about a fucking picnic!' he would yell at his band in later years whenever they began to play it with completely the wrong idea in mind. In fact, it belonged in the same compromised place as earlier future-nostalgic songs like 'I Found A Reason' or 'New Age', only they didn't have Mick Ronson to shine his wondrous light into the gloom.

The album's real tour de force, though, was 'Walk On The Wild Side'. The offhand two-minute acoustic demo that Lou first wrote the year before, with the Broadway musical that never happened in mind, offers only a tiny clue as to the masterpiece it would become on *Transformer*. Struggling to come up with lyrics that suited the original novel's storyline, Lou hadn't even bothered trying to revive it in time for his first solo album. Now, though, by abandoning everything but the title and the street-hustling riff, and repopulating the lyrics with a series of picaresque Warhol characters, he had the bones of something far more compelling. The irony, though unrealised at the time because of his recognised ties

I'll show you mine if you show me yours. Lou makes his
historic appearance onstage in London at David Bowie's
8 July 1972 show at the Royal Festival Hall. Rhinestone
jacket insisted upon by Angie Bowie. (Getty Images)

'Edith Piaff, he ain't.'
Legendary rock critic
Lester Bang's verdict
on the 'new look'
Lou of the early 70s.
(Getty Images)

The 'Phantom of Rock'
ill at ease before
openly frolicking
English hippies at the
Garden Party festival
at Crystal Palace Bowl,
in September 1973.
(Top: Rex Features/
bottom: Getty Images)

Rock'n'roll Animal. In 1974
Lou Reed adopted his most
outrageous image yet, playing
heavy rock versions of the Velvets
classics and feigning shooting
up onstage. Above: onstage at
the Carre Theatre, Amsterdam.
Left: appearing on the bill at The
Who's show at Charlton Athletic
football ground. (Getty Images)

Radio Ethiopia meets Radio Brooklyn.
Patti Smith and Lou Reed, CBGBs,
New York, 1976. (Getty Images)

By the 1980s grown-up Lou was actually having fun. Below left: performing on the *Legendary Hearts* tour, 1983. (Rex Features)
Below: with second wife Sylvia Morales, outside Jerry's restaurant, New York, October 1984. (Getty Images)

Overleaf: 19 March, 1989, onstage at the St. James Theatre, Manhattan, performing from his game changing new album *New York*. (Getty Images)

with the Factory scene, was how little personal experience Lou Reed had actually had of the very real people he mentions by name throughout the song.

Holly Woodlawn, for example, who crops up in the very first verse as the drag queen from Miami who shaved her legs so then 'he was a she', was astounded the first time she heard the song, while riding in the back of a yellow taxi cab. 'I met him once at a party at the Factory!' she would later complain. 'We didn't have intimate relations…' It was the same for Joe Dallesandro, who said he never knew Lou and that the 'Little Joe' character evoked in the song who 'never once gave it away' was entirely derived from the seedy characters he played in Warhol movies like *Flesh* and *Trash*. The Sugar Plum Fairy was no more than a drug dealer from San Francisco Lou had once come across and just liked the name of, thought it would sound good in a song one day, which it did.

None of which really mattered. It was the dark, forbidden milieu these characters suggested that really worked for the millions who now became switched on to Lou Reed via 'Walk On The Wild Side'. What really clinched the deal, though, was the music, the production. With the guitar used only sparingly, and Lou's ghostly vocals slowed to almost spoken word, Bowie and Ronson used all the space that was left to weave in the kind of colours unheard till then outside the more inventive film soundtracks. The walking upright bass supplied by Blue Mink's Herbie Flowers – subtly augmented by a double-tracked electric bass, also played by Flowers – was the real star of the show. As were the doo-doo-doo backing vocals that served as a sort of chorus supplied by the Thunderthighs (the British vocal trio of Karen Friedman, Dari

Lalou and Casey Synge). Again, though, what really lifted the song up into a whole other realm was the string arrangement written by Ronson – gossamer light it adds bruised flesh to the spidery hipster swagger of the rest of the song. Then, just when it seems impossible to ladle any more cream onto the cake, that rich, smoky baritone sax – played by Bowie's old sax teacher, the veteran jazzer Ronnie Ross – comes in with just 40 seconds of the track to go, but begins gradually fading after just 20, adding the final visceral touch to a demi-monde that can barely stand the pain of its own feelings.

Every other track on *Transformer* had its own, diamond-in-the-dirt back story – the ode to his former mentor, 'Andy's Chest', its shuddering reference to his shooting by Valerie Solanas belied by the breathtaking, tumbling poetry which follows; the sublime 'Make Up', considered another witty joke about hes that are shes at the time but actually another irony-free paean to all the different kinds of love Lou had now encountered, its 'We're coming out / Out of our closets / Out on the streets' taken of course from his personal experience of the Stonewall protests; the brilliantly parodic 'New York Telephone Conversation', sung in parallel with Bowie's amusingly lisping co-respondent; the straight not straight rockers like 'Hanging Around' and 'I'm So Free', Ronno trading guitar licks with Lou's verbal pricks like it was never in style in the first place. But it was 'Walk On The Wild Side' that everyone would remember. Or rather, that no one – least of all Lou Reed – would ever be allowed to forget.

The other thing that would make *Transformer* such a conversation piece when it was released in November 1972 was the cover: the now famous black-and-white sleeve-front image of Lou in a rhinestone jacket bought for him by Angie Bowie, the white pancaked face and black panda-eyes that looked so wretched in real life now made fabulously glamorous under the lasciviously gazing lens, the picture framed by the thin cloud of gold across the top and the artfully applied green and red pencil-stripe that outlines his partially hidden guitar. The shot was taken by the London-based photographer Mick Rock, whom Bowie had introduced him to. With Lou and Bettye then staying at a flat in Wimbledon, Rock had become a frequent visitor, befriending the musician and accompanying him on many of his nocturnal ramblings through Soho, which Lou loved for its resemblance to afterhours life in Greenwich Village, but without the constant threat of violence and screaming police sirens. 'Lou,' Rock concluded, 'was a creature of the netherworld.' His pictures of him should reflect that. The shot on the cover of *Transformer* came from the very first show Lou did on his own in London, at the King's Cross Cinema, just days before beginning work at Trident on *Transformer*. Recalling the occasion in *Time* magazine, in the wake of Lou's death, Rock recalled the shot as 'a taste of magic whose potency was instant and totally in synch with Lou's art, and whose magic has never dimmed'. It became the defining image of Lou Reed, capturing forever who Lou was, whether he agreed or not, in the rest of the world's mind's eye.

It was the images on the back of the *Transformer* cover, though, that have continued to intrigue and titillate audiences over the years. On the left: a wonderfully outré drag queen in a splendid wig and fabulous dress slitted up to the crotch. On the right: what might be her beau: a très butch bit of beefcake dressed in tight white T-shirt and even tighter blue jeans, with what appears to be a horse's cock stuffed down the front (and side). For a long time the rumours were that these were both pictures of Lou Reed, depicting the two sides of his sexuality. In fact, this was Lou's friend Ernie Thormahlen. 'We just put a banana down there.' He added with a smirk.

In the lead-up to the album's release, Lou did a full-scale UK tour with The Tots. By now the hype machine was beginning to kick into high gear and there were unkind ripplings in the music press, both sniffing that this was just the latest passing fancy of Bowie's and that Lou Reed was a fad which would be finished before it gained any real headway. Even those who got it, like Nick Kent in the *NME*, were now leaning far more to that other American refugee whose career Bowie was making such a big show of resurrecting: Iggy Pop.

Certainly live onstage, Pop and his recently reconstituted Stooges had the edge. Where Iggy had taken the mythology of the rock'n'roll rebel one step further, appearing shirtless onstage, ripping at his own flesh with broken glass, even walking out, messiah-like, across the upraised hands of his hysterical young audience, Lou was still ambling around the stage like the pudgy Uncle Fester of the family, his band The Tots taken about as seriously as their stupid name. Still seen as more ghoul than cool, Lou, it seemed, could not escape the idea that he was Bowie's protégé now, no longer the other way around.

That was a perception that would change sharply, however, after *Transformer* was released – and with it the songs that would utterly transform Lou Reed's career. First, though, Lou would have to endure a further death by a thousand cuts from reviewers who, unconvinced by what they saw as his desperate embrace of the glam rock Bowie was then accused of introducing, without being asked first, now turned against Lou Reed in earnest. Leading the backlash in Britain was the *NME*, whose Charles Shaar Murray characterised *Transformer* in his review as 'a collection of songs witty, songs trivial, songs dull, songs gay, songs sad, none of them really much cop'.

It was in America, though, where Lou and Bettye returned home, in time for its release, that the knives were really out. The *New Yorker* called the album 'lame, pseudo-decadent lyrics, lame pseudo-something-or-other singing, and a just plain lame band'. Henry Edwards also panned the album in the *New York Times*. While *Rolling Stone* writer Nick Tosches highlighted just four 'quality' songs on the album, dismissing the rest as 'artsy-fartsy kind of homo stuff'. Or why, in the wake of the success that *Transformer* brought him, one of the staunchest supporters of the Velvet Underground, the legendary *Creem* editor, Lester Bangs, would write: 'He's the guy who gave dignity and poetry and rock'n'roll to smack, speed, homosexuality, sado-masochism, murder, misogyny, stumblebum passivity and suicide – and then proceeded to belie his achievements and return to the mire by turning the whole thing into a monumental bad joke.'

Despite such caustic wit, the powers that be at RCA in New York and London were delighted with the way *Transformer* had turned out, feeling there might be as many as two hit singles on there. It was Bowie, though, who tipped them off to the potential of 'Walk On The Wild Side' being a flag-bearer. Lou didn't see it at all. Sick with worry that it would go the way of so many of his previous releases and get banned by radio, it was only when David spoke to him personally and told him what an opportunity he might be missing if he didn't go with what he knew and allow RCA to release 'Walk On The Wild Side' as a single that Lou finally relented, reasoning to himself: the reviews of the album had been so awful, what's the worst that could happen?

6
Suicide City

Lou Reed finally became a big rock'n'roll star in the spring of 1973, when 'Walk On The Wild Side' reached No. 16 in the US charts, and, off the back of that, tiptoed like the boogie man into the UK Top 10. This despite being a song explicitly about cross-dressing transsexuals, who shoot so much speed they think they're 'James Dean for a day', though never lose their heads even when 'giving head', but who periodically use Valium to 'help that crash.' In America where 'giving head' was a familiar term, RCA issued a specially edited version of the single, which bleeped out the offending words. Partly because of the resulting notoriety that afforded the single, 'Walk On The Wild Side' became the No. 1 jukebox hit in America that summer, everyone from beer-quaffing truckers to cigarette-munching speed freaks feeding their nickels and dimes into record machines all over the country.

In Britain, where the crusty upper echelons of the good old BBC had no idea that it wasn't only women who plucked their eyebrows or shaved their legs, let alone what people like that might do with their heads while 'speeding away', didn't even blink their eyes when Radio One's then lunchtime jock Johnnie Walker announced 'Walk On The Wild Side' as his Record of the Week, spinning it every day to millions of listeners around the UK, almost all of whom didn't pick up on the drugs or sex references either. Walker was an album-oriented ex-pirate-radio DJ who liked to keep his freak flag flying by squeezing onto his otherwise anodyne playlist the kinds of records fellow daytime DJs at the station would never have dreamed of. He did the same later that year with Steve Miller's 'The Joker' (nobody at the Beeb got the 'midnight toker' reference in that, either). But that single had flopped due to poor distribution. 'Walk On The Wild Side' had no such problems, and RCA capitalised on its chart success by gleefully running the first of their Phantom of Rock adverts in all the music papers – a sobriquet Lou Reed was to more than live up to over the coming years, though not at all in the way RCA might have hoped.

So while Lou Reed was rewarded for this by seeing 'Walk On The Wild Side' become one of the signature songs of the year, he had already made up his mind never to make another album like it. By then he had also decided never to work with David Bowie again, either. 'He hated being in Bowie's shadow,' the late Stiv Bators would tell me in 1980. Stiv had got to know Lou, briefly, he claimed, during the days when his band, The Dead Boys, played at New York's premier punk club, CBGBs. 'I asked him about that,' he said, staring at me through the kind of wraparound sunglasses Lou had made famous a decade before. 'He felt like Bowie had stolen from him, and that was okay, but now people were saying Lou was ripping Bowie off and that he couldn't fucking stand!'

For his part, Bowie couldn't see what was so obvious to everyone in Lou's immediate circle. When, on his *Aladdin Sane* album, released in April 1973, just as *Transformer* was also peaking in the charts, Bowie sang, in the track 'Cracked Actor', 'since he pinned you baby you're a porcupine', Lou recognised it as yet another 'borrowing' from his own street argot, drug slang he'd developed with John Cale. 'Pinning someone meant they were on drugs,' Cale explained to Paul Trynka. 'You'd pinned them. You'd got them.'

Lou began to feel like Bowie had pinned him good and it was time to show the world there was more to scary old Lou Reed than merely being one of the many shades of Bowie's eye shadow. In an interview with *Circus* magazine, he had even described Bowie as 'a very nasty person, actually'. Others who were there claim Lou was just insanely jealous of Bowie's still escalating success, of how easily David seemed to navigate his way through the pitfalls of the business, never once missing a trick. If so, this was Lou's paranoia at its worst. Little did he apparently know that with his finances in disarray and a backing band that was on the point of open rebellion, Bowie was already plotting his own way out of the Ziggy phase of his career; a wonderfully theatrical bit of rock'n'roll suicide on stage at the Hammersmith Odeon scheduled for 3 July, where he would make his now famous 'resignation speech'.

Asked 30 years later to recall his feelings about that time, Reed was plainly still fidgety on the subject, claiming he didn't even feel any sense of triumph or even satisfaction when 'Walk On The Wild Side' blindsided the censor, at least in the UK, to become his first legitimate hit single.

'I, you know… I'm not amused by the situation at all, but that anyone would… You know, in books you [had] *Naked Lunch* and Allen Ginsberg. In movies you [had] God knows what. Who could possibly be bothered by the lyrics to "Wild Side"? It's inconceivable.' He said he was offended at the very idea that anyone would find his lyrics offensive. 'I mean, it is just so offensive that it's not amusing.' But the whole glam rock Bowie association that came with it, because of that did the song become something of a millstone for him? 'No, because without it, who knows, maybe I'd be digging a ditch somewhere. So thank God for it.' End of subject.

The ramifications of suddenly being bracketed in the same realm of rock stardom as Bowie – and those others that followed in his comet trail in 1973: Roxy Music, Mott The Hoople, Iggy & the Stooges, Alice Cooper, et al – left Lou Reed conflicted, though. In February, he seemed to celebrate his new, much longed for status as genuine rock'n'roll star by marrying Bettye at home on Long Island. Exactly none of his Warhol-era friends were invited. He then immediately set out with The Tots on what would be his most prestigious tour yet. Suddenly it seemed the whole world wanted Lou Reed to come visit – just as long as he brought his Phantom of Rock costume with him.

By the time Lou Reed arrived back in London at the end of June 1973, to begin recording his next album – the first to carry the full weight of expectation that comes with having to follow up your first hit record with another, equally successful release – a combination of wanting to prove he was not just another grateful member of the Bowie hit-machine and the crushing insecurity that greeted his decision to go it alone without the production team that had rescued his whole life and career left Lou in bad shape. It wasn't just the speed and downers he was using to keep him going now, he'd begun falling back into heroin again. As a result, his four-month-old marriage to Bettye was in even worse shape. 'My lady was a real asshole,' he blurted stoned to one writer. He'd taken to 'bouncing her around', he said.

He'd also begun listening a lot lately to John Lennon's 1970 *Plastic Ono Band* album. The first musical fruits of the former Beatle's primal scream therapy specifically address childhood issues and psychological disorders; in particular, Lou told Bruce Pollock, the opening track, 'Mother', with its haunting opening lines.

'"Mother" by John Lennon,' said Lou. 'That was a song that had realism. I mean, that did it to you. That's about the only [album] I can think of on that level. When I first heard it I didn't even know it was him. I just said: "Who the fuck is that? I don't believe that." Because the lyrics to that are real. You see, he wasn't kidding around. He got right down to it, as down as you can get. I like that in a song.'

Reed now planned to do something similar but in his own voice. Realising, though, that he still needed someone in the studio he could rely on to put flesh on the bones of his ideas, he turned to the 24-year-old Bob Ezrin, then one of the hottest producers in America, due to his series of million-selling album successes with the Alice Cooper band. A multi-talented keyboardist from Canada, Ezrin had produced, mixed and co-written all the best material of Alice Cooper's career – including both the *School's Out* and, most recently, *Billion Dollar Babies* albums. A talented, intelligent man who would go on to work side by side with Roger Waters on the Pink Floyd masterwork, *The Wall*, Ezrin was looking for a project that would establish his credentials as a producer capable of more than the schlock-rock Alice Cooper purveyed. When a proposal to work with Lou Reed on the follow-up to *Transformer* – the most intriguing album of the year – came his way he grabbed at it with both hands.

Ezrin became even more excited as Reed outlined his plans for the album. This would most definitely not be *Transformer II*. Nor would there be a handy catch-all track like 'Walk On The Wild Side'. Rather this would be like that – an album populated by similar demi-monde characters – but on a much larger, far more real scale. No more Andy Warhol caricatures, but real, fucked-up people stuck in a doomed marriage, dominated by speed and dope and whoring themselves out for money, one in which their children are eventually taken away and the wife sees the only way out as suicide. Or put another way, the exact opposite of what any other remotely sane rock star would have chosen to do at the very moment they had, after nearly a decade of trying and failing, finally found a place for themselves at rock's high table.

Ezrin was overjoyed; suggesting what they would make together would amount to 'a film for the ear'. RCA were horrified, seeing it as career suicide. But Lou was insistent. And as the man who was then riding high in the world's charts with the most controversial hit of the year, it was hard for the label to argue. Nevertheless, they would only sanction the recording, they eventually decided, on condition that Reed return the favour by delivering another album in the style of *Transformer* next time around. Better than that, an overjoyed Reed fired back, he would deliver them another *Transformer*, plus a live album packed with all the best bits of his solo and Velvets days. So it was that Lou Reed began recording the album, *Berlin*, that would both become his masterpiece and effectively end his career as a major recording star.

Recorded, coincidentally, at Morgan Studios in north London, the site of Lou's failed solo debut two years before, like that album Ezrin began by putting together a team of crack session players. This time, though, with a much bigger budget to play with, Ezrin recruited top-drawer players like the bassist Jack Bruce, late of Cream; the drummers Aynsley Dunbar, fresh from Frank Zappa's band, and B. J. Wilson, of Procul Harum; the keyboardists Steve Winwood, still then of Traffic, and Blue Weaver, then of the Strawbs; the highly respected Brecker brothers, Randy and Michael, on trumpet and tenor sax, respectively; with Bob also supplying piano and mellotron, as well as production. Ezrin also made a bold move by flying over from Los Angeles the guitarists Steve Hunter and Dick Wagner, both highly skilled players whom Bob had used to great effect behind the scenes on the last two Alice Cooper albums.

Others were brought in on an ad hoc basis, but that was the core outfit which would provide the unusual soundtrack to Lou's 'film for the ear'. Leaving Lou to strum his acoustic guitar and sing. If you could call it that…

Aynsley Dunbar, speaking to me in 2006, recalled his experience of working on *Berlin* as 'one of the strangest of my career'. He explained: 'Jack Bruce was the bass player on that album and so it was good to play with him again.

Berlin was a very depressing album though – interesting but *very* depressing. I believe Lou [was] doing heroin, and what came out of it was depression.' Strangest of all, he remembered, was when 'David Bowie called me one day and invited me down to his final show with the Spiders From Mars [at the Hammersmith Odeon, on 3 July], which turned out to be the famous one where he made his "retirement" speech. He wanted me to sit in on a couple of numbers. Lou Reed had the night off and I asked Bowie: "Do you want me to bring Lou?" He said: "Well, that's up to you." So I called Lou and told him about it and he said: "Oh, I'm calling a session tonight." But we didn't do a damn thing. It was just to stop me going to the gig. I don't know why, they were having an argument or something. But I dragged Lou to the party afterwards and there's this famous picture of us sitting together at this long table, David and Lou and me in the middle. Jagger and Jeff Beck were there too. In the end, Lou wanted me to be his musical director but I couldn't handle the attitude and stuff.'

Miraculously, given this backdrop, the songs on *Berlin* were among the best, most affecting Reed would ever write. As with both his previous solo albums, the backbone of this 'film of the ear' comprised a handful of older songs, some dating back again as far as the Velvets. Beginning with the atmospheric title track, which Lou filched from *Lou Reed*, but reconfigured here with Ezrin into a much more cinematic piece that sets the distinctly downbeat tone of the entire set, it was hard not to picture Lou, 'the Sinatra of the 70s', as Nick Kent had memorably recently described him in the *NME*, slumped on a bar stool, dragging on a cigarette as he whispered his way through the verses like a man on crutches making his way slowly down an alley.

After the smoke-ringed prologue to the story of Jim and Caroline, two speed freak junkies clinging to each other more in desperation than hope, not quite reconciled to their fates but going down fast, finding new depths of despair with every wrong turn in the road, we first meet Caroline in 'Lady Day', stumbling in and out of Berlin bars, then home to the hotel she and Jim live in with its 'greenish walls' and 'bathroom in the hall', the band lumbering along, as if behind her. 'Men Of Good Fortune', which follows, gives us Jim's perspective, comparing his lot to those with rich daddies to fall back on, at the same time concluding, 'Me, I just don't care at all.'

And so the story goes on. In 'Caroline Says I', Jim bemoans the way Caroline, who whores herself out for money they both spend on drugs, talks of him of being 'just a toy' when what she really wants is a man, comparing her to poison in a vial at the same time as lauding her as his 'Germanic Queen'. Caroline responds in 'How Do You Think It Feels', taunting Jim by reminding him she's the one who 'always makes love by proxy', usually after she's been up for five days 'speeding and lonely'. 'Oh Jim' follows, full of rage and violence and dreams pulverised.

All the while the music is both impassioned and restrained, tasteful but hard as nails, orchestral in places, oboes, strings, horns, like an off-off-Broadway musical without the laughs, the curtains parting occasionally to allow a fiery guitar solo to break loose, the drums and bass as taut as a tripwire. But if side one was harrowing, side two of *Berlin* was devastating. The story resumes

with 'Caroline Says II', as she picks herself up off the
floor after another savage beating from Jim, daring him to
hit her again, it won't matter, because she simply doesn't
love him any more. The most agonising moment on the
album, and its longest track, is the almost too painful to
bear 'The Kids', which begins: 'They're taking her children
away...', then goes on to detail Caroline's serial infideli-
ties and rampant drug abuse, as though only the mother
bears the responsibility for the rearing of their children.
It's stark, grisly, thoroughly depressing stuff which reaches
its blood-freezing denouement with the sound of small
children howling in despair, calling out for their mummy.
On the next track, 'The Bed', a glacial first-hand account
by Jim of Caroline's subsequent suicide, Reed's whispering
voice intones the bed's history as the place where their
children were conceived, where they slept and where she
finally 'cut her wrists that odd and fateful night'. When
the music goes into a deep, haunting swoon at the end it
becomes an endurance test, the listener practically begging
for a shard of light to somehow relieve the unremitting
darkness, before finally it comes in the climactic closer, the
all too aptly named – one prays non-ironic – 'Sad Song'.
Even there, though, as the strings strive to lift the feeling
towards something cathartic, Steve Hunter's beautiful guitar
break aiming for something higher, Lou doesn't let you off
the hook, as Jim concludes: 'Somebody else would have
broken both of her arms.'

Considering where Lou Reed had spent his entire musical
career – in the backrooms of the music biz, making records
for the doomed to gaze at their reflections in – the subject

matter of *Berlin* is arguably in keeping with the arc of his own artistic narrative. Yet considering he was now coming off the back of a bona fide, all-comers-welcome worldwide hit, it's staggering how prepared he was to risk it all for an album, masterpiece though it is, as profoundly disenchanted as *Berlin*. That while shrewd David Bowie was busy releasing crowd-pleasers like *Aladdin Sane*, Lou Reed would almost deliberately sabotage his own career in the name of... what? Art? Arrogance? Disdain? That and more?

Certainly, *Berlin* would be a major puzzlement for those who would be tasked with reviewing it when it was released in October 1973. In a year when rock goliaths like Pink Floyd would release their own life–madness–death concept album, *The Dark Side Of The Moon*, and The Who would produce the self-referential life–madness–rebirth double album *Quadrophenia*; when groups relatively new to the charts like Genesis, Roxy Music, Cockney Rebel and Queen would purport to release albums that spoke of a world denuded of its 1960s innocence, with music that had gone through rock's looking glass and returned bearing previously unheard of gifts – *Berlin* was by far the most searching, emotionally, the most challenging, musically, of its audience – and the most monumentally despised and misunderstood.

Reviewing it for *NME*, Nick Kent, one of the few contemporary writers to see *Berlin* for what it was, 'a coup', hit the nail on the head when he concluded: 'The record's immediate effect is more akin to watching, say, *Last Tango In Paris*, than... a new Rolling Stones album.' It was in large part thanks to this recommendation from the man then widely considered the most fashionable rock writer of his generation, plus the overspill of fan recognition engendered by the success of *Transformer* earlier that same year, that *Berlin* reached No. 7 in the UK album chart. Though it didn't hang around for long once word spread of the album's deeply tormented soul. Indeed, it would be 20 years before another Lou Reed album got a sniff of the UK Top 10.

In America it was a very different story, and several reviewers reacted furiously to *Berlin*. Writing in *Rolling Stone*, Stephen Davis led the charge by declaring the album so 'patently offensive' that one wished to take 'physical vengeance' on any artist that would consider recording such a dreadful thing. While in *Creem* Robert Christgau refused to be shocked, but was merely bored. He said that the story was lousy and if 'something similar was coughed up by some avant-garde asshole' everyone would be then 'too bored to puke at it.' He gave it a C. In response, sales were abysmal, and while *Transformer* would eventually sell more than a million copies there, *Berlin* only just managed to dig its dirty fingernails into the US Hot 100, going belly-up at a paltry No. 98.

So dispiriting was the media backlash to *Berlin* that plans Lou and Bob had discussed for a possible stage adaptation of the album – this, lest we forget, was the era of theatrical live rock show productions – were put on hold indefinitely. In fact, it would be another 34 years before that dream came true, by which time the vast critical reappraisal of *Berlin* had begun. Far too late to save the original release from the odium it would engender for years to come in Reed's career. For the rest of the 1970s it seemed no interview would be complete without forcing Lou to reflect on the folly of his grand gesture. On occasion, he would be bold, unrepentant, sure of its place in history. 'Oh, *Berlin* will see its place in the sun some day,' he told the late British writer Caroline Coon, in 1976. 'It's better than all [my] albums.' He even insisted he was shocked at the immensity of critical opprobrium that met the album. 'But who cares about critics? *Berlin* was an album for adults. I want to make real albums. That whole thing started because I wanted to write real songs about something that was relevant.' At the time of its release three years before, though, when Bruce Pollock asked if he intended writing any more albums like *Berlin*, he demurred: 'I think I've gone as deep as I want to go for my own mental health. If I got any deeper I'd wind up disappearing.' Pollock certainly didn't foresee a long career for the singer. 'I figured he'd go the way of most Andy Warhol superstars,' he admits now, 'to an early drug overdose.'

When Ian Fortnam quizzed him about *Berlin* exactly 30 years later, however, wondering aloud where all that darkness had come from, pointing out the lack, for example, of even a twilit 'Perfect Day', to break up the gloom, Lou merely shrugged. 'I have no idea. It was just getting together with Ezrin, we wanted to do what we were calling a movie for the mind and it grew out of that idea. But when you say there is no "Perfect Day" on there, well don't be too sure about that... melodically there certainly is, arrangement-wise there certainly is. The key to "Perfect Day" is the last line: "You made me forget myself, I thought I was someone else, someone good, and you're gonna reap what you sow." So going from there to "Berlin" is not a big leap. Actually, you could put that right in there without a problem, probably after "Oh Jim".'

But what prompted such darkness at a time when his career seemed so full of starlight? 'Well, it's not let's sit up and dance and be happy, but it's like, I prefer to think of it as a Bergman movie or a Kuwosawa movie. You know it's not "Hey, hey, hey, yippy-doo", it's more film noir. Which … I guess that lets Kurosawa out, but when I say Kurosawa I mean intensity, or in *Rashomon* depending how you look at it. That's the reference points for me, if you know what I'm talking about.' He paused, then added dryly: 'Boy meets girl, boy gets girl, boy loses girl and then it stops.'

'Girls slashes wrists' isn't normally something you'd expect to find in the equation, though, Fortnam persisted. 'Well, of course it's not what you normally expect, but that's the point… I mean, you have so many records that go the other way and here is a chance to move you emotionally, physically – remember what I was saying – *physically* move you, and *emotionally* move you. You know, you're not expecting it, you know, because you don't get that.'

Why had he specifically chosen Berlin as the setting for Caroline and Jim's story, though? 'It was simply that Berlin was a divided city, and it was cosmopolitan and a very sophisticated city. It was the home of German film noir and expressionism and I wanted this to be the city in which this little plot takes place, and it was emblematic that it was a divided city.'

Speaking online in 2012, Bob Ezrin told the Greek website channel.com that as far as he was concerned the only problem with Berlin was that 'it was ahead of its time,' pointing out that subjects like 'spousal abuse, suicide, speed addiction' are these days the daily conversations of reality TV, but back in 1973 much of this was still considered seriously taboo, at least in the arts.

In that context, it's tempting to wonder what direction Lou Reed's career might have taken had *Berlin* been heralded as the masterpiece it is now regarded as 40 years later. Might Lou Reed have become the Stephen Sondheim of suicide, sexploitation and drug despair? In the event, it would be a decade before Lou Reed would ever again attempt anything on the scale of *Berlin*. Instead, he now went off in completely the opposite direction, as if punishing both his record company, his fans and the critics for ever doubting him. They preferred all that cute *Transformer* is-it-a-he-or-an-it stuff. What he called all that 'negative punk' stuff. Well, now they could have it…

The next two years would find Lou Reed completely out of control. He was perpetually at loggerheads with RCA, who lost no time in reminding him that he now owed them at least one more conventional glam rock album and one live album – a promise that Lou, typically, had never foreseen actually having to keep, so convinced was he that *Berlin* would be an even bigger hit than *Transformer*. His marriage to Bettye was now over, as he effectively spent the next two years either touring the world or getting wasted in the studio making albums that were so filled with contempt for their audience, but mostly for himself, the creature he had sunk to, that when his deal with RCA finally came to an end in 1975 they couldn't wait to get rid of him.

Because worldwide sales of *Berlin* had been such 'a total disaster', he told Caroline Coon, 'The record company did a quick scurry around like little bunnies. But I went somnambulant. It wasn't brain rot like some people think. I just kinda did no more.'

The first evidence of this new somnambulance was the live album, *Rock'n'Roll Animal*, released in February 1974. Recorded at the Academy of Music, in New York, on 21 December 1973, and featuring no longer The Tots but a top-drawer backing group culled from the best available talent in the New York session gene pool, including both Steve Hunter and Dick Wagner, the guitarist from the *Berlin* sessions band, the moustached Indian-Canadian bassist Prakash John, the former Don McLean keyboardist Ray Colcord, and the former Mandala drummer Pentti 'Whitey' Glan. With the exceptions of Hunter and Wagner, whose duelling guitars dominated the new, rock-steady live sound, none of the new Lou Reed band had any connection whatsoever to any of the music he had made in the past. They were simply top musicians playing for pay and doing it exceptionally well – if you liked your rock hard, heavy and spiced up with some deft musical chops that would not have sounded out of place on a Doobie Brothers or early Steely Dan record. Given material to handle as febrile as old Velvets classics like 'White Light/White Heat' though, or – look away now – 'Heroin', the sound verged on musical heresy. Even Lou, who in his permanently stoned mood could dig just about anything on a technical level, would later call it 'bad Velvet Underground'. Even the applause on the live album had to be manufactured to a degree, after it was discovered a mike had failed during the actual concert. Hence a lot of the applause on *Rock'n'Roll Animal* comes from a John Denver concert! The extra applause one hears as Lou walks on the stage to start singing 'Sweet Jane' is not actual on-the-night audience rapture but the result of the producer turning up a knob later in the studio.

With a set that some nights included as many as eight old Velvet Underground songs in a set that never included more than 14 songs, leaving just three from *Berlin* and three from *Transformer*, the single live album came with just five tracks: four extended versions of 'Sweet Jane', 'Heroin', 'White Light/ White Heat' and 'Rock 'n' Roll', and 'Lady Day'. Many at the time saw the whole enterprise as another sick Lou Reed joke, a kind of post-irony irony set to trap the cash-register minds of the record company and those too young or foolish not to have an inkling about where these songs actually came from. Speaking to Barney Hoskyns in 1996, however, Lou insisted that was not the case at all. 'To record songs you'd written four years earlier and have them get popular now? That was pretty interesting. And not to play guitar on them? That was very painful. But *Rock'n'Roll Animal* is still one of the best live recordings ever done. I've got enough distance on it now that I can hear it today. Those songs were made for that. And there's also a vibe on there that's – phew!'

Speaking in 2003, Lou claimed he was influenced by Mitch Ryder's earlier razzed-up version of 'Rock 'n' Roll' – coincidentally, produced by Bob Ezrin. 'I said: "Aha, that's fun." So Ezrin got Alice Cooper's band for me. I can't play that way, I don't wanna play that way, but they were as good at "that way" as anybody else around, so I said: "Okay, here's the material." They didn't know it from the Velvet Underground, they'd never heard it, so I just taught them all the whole thing again. Like, now we'll try it again, see what happens five years later. Duh. Let's see if [the audience] get it this time around. Change the presentation. I mean, it is not something that I would want to keep doing, but it was probably one of the greatest live records ever made. So there you have it.'

According to the live album's producer, Steve Katz – former member of Blood, Sweat & Tears and brother to Lou's manager, Dennis – it was actually he who first planted the seed in Lou's mind. Speaking with the website bedfordandbowery.com in 2013, Katz related how he'd first met Lou at Dobbs Ferry rehearsal studio in New York, where Lou was still licking his wounds after the critical drubbing of *Berlin*. Steve, who liked Reed as a person and greatly admired the huge chance he'd taken making an albumn like *Berlin*, suggested to his brother that maybe the way back was to take the best of the Velvet Underground songs, throw in some of *Berlin* and *Transformer*, put a proper kick-ass American band behind him, rather than The Tots who he was still using at that point, and start slaying audiences again. Then release a proper blood-to-the-head live album of the back of it. When Dennis and Lou got excited by the idea, they suggested that maybe Steve could produce such an album, an opportunity he leapt at. 'I wanted to get back to my rock'n'roll roots,' he recalled, 'and Lou was a real rock'n'roll person.'

There were later suggestions, meant kindly no doubt, but by people that had clearly not experienced the full horror of the *Rock'n'Roll Animal* shows, that Lou was simply responding to the new hard rock ethic of life on the American road in the mid-1970s. Even Bowie, who would officially come out of 'retirement' in the summer of 1974, touring his more hard-edged, guitar-driven, ultra-Americanised *Diamond Dogs* revue, seemed to be making concessions to an audience then more used to a steady – and, more the tour promoters' point of view, lucrative – diet of mainstream rock acts like Bad Company, Led Zeppelin, Bachman-Turner Overdrive and the Faces. But while Rod Stewart would be happy to dye his hair California blonde, he would never have thought to crop it concentration-camp short first, then have Iron Crosses shaved into the side of his head, as the newly blond, newly even scarier Lou Reed now did. And while Alice Cooper and David Bowie would make much of their extravagant new theatrical stage productions, only Lou Reed considered tying up his arm with his microphone lead on stage and mimicking taking a shot of smack during 'Heroin', another entertaining new feature of Lou Reed's 1974 'stage show'. Nor did many rock stars find themselves having to be carried on- and offstage some nights by world-weary roadies who thought they'd seen it all and now had to think again.

When the tour reached Australia that summer – eight shows, including three at Sydney's Hordern Pavilion (capacity: 5300), four at Melbourne's Festival Hall (cap: 5400), and one apiece at the Adelaide (cap: 2000) and Brisbane (cap: 4000) versions of the Festival Hall – Lou gave a desultory interview to gathered journalists at the airport that resembled nothing so much as Andy Warhol doing Lou Reed, doing Andy Warhol. The tabloid hacks sniggered, seeing it all as a delicious part of the act, but the reality was less artful. Opening for Reed on that tour was a new up-and-coming young band from Sydney named AC/DC. Their singer at the time, Dave Evans, now claims that '[Reed] was so screwed up he had to get people to help him onto the stage and help him off. I thought: "That's his stage act." But I saw him at breakfast the next morning and he had two people helping him up for breakfast as well! It wasn't a stage act, mate...'

All of which, paradoxically, and to Lou's immense told-you-so satisfaction, worked in his favour for a while. At least, commercially. Not only were ticket sales up, with the cover of *Rock'n'Roll Animal* depicting what looked like Mick Rock's *Transformer* cover shot but coming from the wrong end of the rainbow – the real rock'n'roll Frankenstein revealed! Quick, run for your lives! – sales for the live album more than tripled those of *Berlin*, giving Lou Reed his second gold album in America. A worthwhile stopgap, then, perhaps, before unveiling his next all-original studio masterwork?

Not quite. For the next Lou Reed solo album, *Sally Can't Dance*, would become the second-most reviled of his career – up to that point, at least, though there would be more to come. Recorded in the early spring of 1974, at New York's plush, musician-friendly Electric Lady studios, purpose-built by Jimi Hendrix's old engineer, Eddie Kramer, specifically for artists who required more than a mere recording facility in which to create their great art, and released in August 1974, at the height of blond-Nazi Lou mania, *Sally Can't Dance* became the musical embodiment of everything that Lou Reed's shattered and near-fatally comprised career had come to represent: an album of cynical retreads and glam-rock-by-numbers trash. Zombie rock from the king of rock's walking undead that would also become the biggest hit record he would ever have in America, home of the slave, as Lou saw it. Laugh? He never did any more anyway.

Looking back on those days now, in conversation with Will Hodgkinson of the *Sunday Times*, in September 2013, Lou quipped that his blond cropped hair had made him look 'Like Brando in the *Young Lions*.' Adding, straight-faced: 'Lemme tell ya, that hair wasn't easy.' He said it got him into fights. 'I'd be walking down the street in New York in the 1970s and it was, "Hey, you a fag man?"'

The trouble was, Lou said later, 'I ducked behind the image for so long that after a while there was a real danger of it becoming just a parody thing, where even if I was trying to be serious you didn't know whether to take it seriously or not. There'd been so much posturing that there was a real confusion between that life and real life. I was doing a tightrope act that was pretty scary, no matter *where* you were viewing it. It's not like I didn't know it, I just didn't know how to get out of it.'

The release of *Sally Can't Dance* only buried his public persona even deeper in the mire, despite its crushing success in America, where it reached No. 10, the highest chart position any Lou Reed album would ever attain in his lifetime.

Backed by the same rhythm section as his touring band, but augmented in the studio by the former Iron Butterfly guitarist Danny Weiss, a six-piece horn section, led by Steve Katz, and the newest and most lasting addition to Lou's permanent band, the 27-year-old keyboardist Michael Fonfara, an exquisitely gifted player, writer and arranger who had cut his teeth playing in Buddy Miles's Electric Flag, and would now effectively become musical director of the Lou Reed band, both studio and touring.

Imaginatively produced by Steve Katz, the sound he captured is that of the hip, jive, out-there New York scene of the mid-1970s, after the world and its ugly sister have come out, drugs are now a respectable lifestyle choice, and the only life worth living is the one that begins after midnight. It was just a shame that the songs were so throwaway. With the exception of the cigarette-dangling title track, all fat big-mama horns and frazzled guitars and Lou leering into the mike like only he can, and moments of genuine lyrical and musical vituperation like 'Kill Your Sons', most of *Sally Can't Dance* simply flatters to deceive, right down to the comically parodic cover shot, of a blonde Lou, shades back in place, collar turned up, guitar nowhere to be seen, having now vanished from both his live show and the studio set-up. Like, ooh, who's the scary man, mummy? Oh, no one...

'A record that I really couldn't stand,' is how Lou later described it in an interview with *Sounds* magazine's Sandy Robertson. 'I know people that like me who love that record but... my answer was to make *Metal Machine Music*.' A pause. And then: 'Do you understand what I just said? You have no idea what I just said to you! My answer to having a Top 10 record was to put out an album with no vocal, no...'

No nothing. That's right. Unhappy, apparently, at having blown his chances at sustained commercial success not just once, when he walked out on the Velvet Underground, just as Atlantic Records was gearing up to give the big promotional heave-ho to *Loaded*, nor satiated by the way he so spectacularly booby-trapped his hard-fought eventual stardom with *Transformer*, Lou Reed was out to become the world triple-champion of slamming the door shut on your own success.

And he was going to do it with such style that even his most devoted fans would no longer be able to stomach it.

7
White Noise

In 1975, Lou Reed's metamorphosis into a real live rock'n'roll animal was all but complete. In his review of *Sally Can't Dance*, Robert Christgau, who seemed to like the album despite himself, had observed: 'Even as he shits on us he can't staunch his own cleverness.' Lou took it as a compliment. Hey, hadn't he been the clever one who beat the critics to the punch by including a song on that album called 'Ennui'? As for shitting on people, by February 1975 when part two of the *Rock'n'Roll Animal* set at the Academy was released as *Lou Reed Live*, there was almost no one left he hadn't shit on. And not just poor hapless freaks like his old flame Nico, now so strung out on smack she'd wept with joy when Lou told her *Berlin* was really all about her, then offered to write her a whole new batch of songs for an album he would produce for her. Lou now had a new girlfriend, named Barbara Hodes, who worked in the fashion world and whose chic one-bedroom apartment on Fifth Avenue he would sleep in – when he could be bothered to sleep. But that wasn't where he took Nico, when she arrived from

Paris, where she'd been subsisting since her own solo career had singularly failed to take off. Nico got to sit and watch Lou shoot speed at his own shitty little place on East 52nd Street. For three days. He never did write another song for her, nor did he recall having offered to produce an album for her. After Nico finally fled his gaff, broken up and hysterical, Lou never bothered to get in contact with her again. Ever.

Dennis Katz was another former confidant who Lou now felt deserved the full force of his bitterness and hatred. Despite two big hit albums in *Transformer* and *Sally Can't Dance*, plus the attendant royalties due from lesser but still relatively significant hits around the world like *Berlin* (Britain) and *Rock'n'Roll Animal* (America), Lou Reed was broke. His divorce settlement to Bettye, finally secured at the end of 1973, and his head-in-the-sand lifestyle – not only did he have big wages to pay for his top-of-the-line band but he had his increasingly expensive drug habits to cover – meant he was constantly scrabbling around for cash. Rather than look to himself, though, he blamed Dennis for everything. Dennis was never 'there for me', he would tell anyone that would listen. Yet it was Dennis that had saved his career by signing him to RCA, Dennis who had saved his career by bringing him first David Bowie as a producer and then his brother, Steve. Dennis that had to put up with all his shit on the road. But that, as Steve Katz put it, was 'in Lou's speed period'. He later recalled how sessions at the studio would be booked for mid-afternoons, but that Lou would not turn up until the early hours, by which time the producer and his musicians would all be dog tired, just as Lou, amped up on his latest methadrine fix, would want to get started.

The temporarily reformed Velvet
Underground onstage at the Ahoy,
Rotterdam, 9 June 1993. (Getty
Images)

David Bowie and Lou Reed attending the movie premiere of
Basquiat at the Paris Theater, 31 July 1996. (Getty Images)

Lou Reed with Debbie Harry at the
Tommy Hilfiger Fashion Show, New
York, 1998. (Rex Features)

With wife Laurie Anderson at the
Tribeca Film Festival in New York,
2002. (Rex Features)

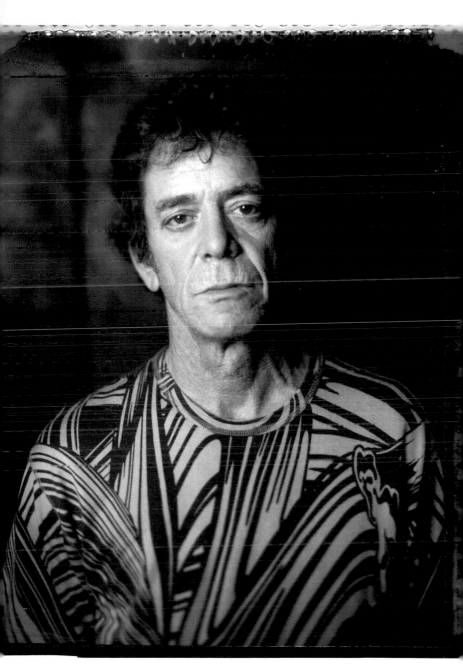
Portrait of Lou. 15 November 2005. (Getty Images)

Lou Reed performs during the DKNY// Jeans Presents Vanity Fair In Concert to benefit the Step Up Women's Network at Irving Plaza, 21 October 2004 in New York City. (Getty Images)

Gorillaz featuring Lou Reed, Glastonbury Festival, 25 June 2010. (Rex Features)

Playing with Metallica in Milan.
13 November 2011. (Rex Features)

In concert at the Auditorium Parco Della
Musica, Rome. 1 March 2006.
(Rex Features)

Performing his album *Berlin*, Royal
Albert Hall, London. 30 June 2008.
(Rex Features)

Lou Reed at *Transformer* book launch,
New York. 3 October 2013. He died
three weeks later. (Rex Features)

The only person who didn't feel the lash of Reed's amphetamine-fuelled barbs was Barbara Hodes. The two had known each other since the mid-1960s, and more meaningfully since the early 1970s, when Barbara was one of the only people Lou used to know who did her best to stay in touch during his 'lost year' working for his father's accountancy firm as a $40-a-week typist. Now even she began to distance herself from her former friend, after spending a harrowing few weeks on tour with him in Europe, where he was doing so much speed he could no longer play the guitar, no longer control his furies, could no longer even smile straight.

But as one more person disappeared from his life like a discarded works, others would appear, more attuned to the high-tension speed vibration Lou now existed on. Mainly speed dealers and other speed freaks. One in particular, Rotten Rita, who sold speed but loved opera, became a favourite. Real name Kenneth Rapp, Rita was another cast-off from Warhol's old Factory scene, a tall, butch guy who claimed he had once been an opera singer and was hung up on Maria Callas. Now living in a dump in Queens, Rita was one of those people you could never be entirely sure of – a big tall ex-con in a dress: one minute generous and giving, the next a potential killer. Lou could relate and would stay up for days with Rita playing her opera records over and over.

Another, more significant other also came into Lou Reed's life at this point: another butch number known simply as Rachel. Real name thought to be Tommy Humphries, Rachel was a half-Mexican-Indian habitué of the New York gay scene in the mid-1970s who affected not to have known or cared who Lou Reed was before she-he met him. Tall and striking-looking, even glamorous when she dressed up, unfortunately her habit of staying up for days with Lou, drinking and speeding and fucking and whatever else they could think of to do and not to do during their intense three-year relationship, meant he could often be found with a three-day-old stubble, sunken eyes and deathly pallor. In a contemporary article for *Creem*, Lester Bangs was one of the first writers to give a thumbnail sketch of Lou Reed's new love. '[L]ong dark hair, bearded, tits, grotesque, abject... like something that might have grovelingly scampered in when Lou opened the door to get milk or papers in the morning.' He later added: 'If the album *Berlin* was melted down and reshaped in human form, it would be this creature.' Bangs, whose incendiary head-to-head encounters with Reed would become the stuff of legend in the 1970s, would later offer his apologies to Lou, declaring the piece one of the few things he ever regretted writing. But Lou never forgave him. Rachel was far too important to him.

They had met in a late-night club in the Village. As Mick Rock later recounted in an interview he gave to *Bambi* magazine, Lou, who had been up for days as usual, recalled Rachel 'wearing this amazing make-up and dress' and belonging to 'a different world to anyone else in the place'. Enraptured, the two repaired to Lou's apartment, where, speeding out of his mind, Lou didn't stop speaking for hours while Rachel sat opposite him 'saying nothing'. Rachel had apparently never heard any of Lou's music – which seems unlikely in that scene but that's what she said, nor did she even know who Lou Reed was, which seems even more unlikely, yet one has to admire her style, realising no doubt how often he was used to being fawned over by people he'd picked up in a club. Reed, who thought he'd seen it all, was hooked. Rachel was simply 'something else'.

Rachel would become such an important presence in Lou Reed's life they became inseparable for the next three years, living together in Lou's tiny two-bed apartment or out on the road, staying in expensive hotels, being photographed together by Mick Rock for a 'fashion spread' in *Penthouse*, or simply hanging out while Lou was being interviewed. An aura began to build up around the couple, with fans and critics alike speculating out loud on the nature of the relationship. Was Rachel just another drag queen? No. The Warhol drag queens affected to be womanly, albeit in a quasi-subversive way; Rachel did not pretend to act like a woman, nor even much dress like one, although she wore her dark hair long and used make-up on her face, and was clearly the feminine companion in the relationship, if you had to be so specific. Was he a transsexual then? Again, probably not. Although it was later rumoured that Rachel 'hated' his cock, there is no evidence that he'd actually had it removed. Besides, Lou loved Rachel's cock. What then? Well, that was nobody's business. This was New York in the mid-1970s, what did any of it matter anyway? Of course they would fight. Lou fought with everyone all the time. And Rachel had her own trip going on when it came to putting up a fight, once flooding out a floor of the Ritz in London when she forgot to turn off the taps. She said, dark eyebrows arched like stilettos. The main thing was Rachel made Lou happy at a time in his life when happiness seemed like an antiquated concept invented by straights to disqualify people like Lou and Rachel from a world they had no intention of being a part of anyway.

When *Lou Reed Live* picked up decent reviews – including a rave from Paul Nelson in *Rolling Stone*, who compared the band's playing to 'near-royal Eric Clapton opulence' before deciding, '[Lou Reed] is still one of a handful of American artists capable of the spiritual home run. Should he put it all together again, watch out' – Lou, who always affected to despise rock critics yet read each and all of his press clippings with a speed freak's cold, brittle eye for detail, was both secretly pleased and filled with disdain. Interviewed by his old Factory friend, Danny Fields, for a piece in *Gig* magazine, Lou quipped: 'This is fantastic – the worse I am, the more it sells. If I wasn't on the record at all next time around, it would probably go to Number One.'

It seemed like a typically self-regarding Reed joke at the time. No one could have guessed how close to the truth it would actually turn out to be. In fact, not only would the next Lou Reed album – the double-disc *Metal Machine Music* – contain no lyrics, or singing, but it would contain no musical instruments either. Not unless you counted a shit-storm of feedback distortion and high-frequency noise that lasted an hour and shredded the nerves like fingernails scraping down a blackboard. Each side was timed to last exactly 16 minutes and 1 second, with the additional gimmick on side four of a final groove in the vinyl that stuck so that the album theoretically never ended – until whatever poor saps had actually sat through it finally roused themselves from a state of catatonia long enough to remove the needle manually.

One horrified RCA executive described it as 'torture music.' But Lou played it all with a straight face, claiming he'd been composing the 'score' for over five years, based on classical themes, avant-garde experimentation and new sonic laws that he had personally subscribed. At various times he claimed the music had given women orgasms, sent men running from the room shitting their pants, and caused rapture among the certifiably insane, and that it was 'the closest I've ever come to perfection'. When Lester Bangs, never slow to inform any passing emperors of the shocking state of their new clothes, took Lou to task about the album in the latest of their bruising press face-offs, Lou snapped: 'I don't make records for fucking flower children.' When a deadpan Lester responded by inquiring if Lou had ever tried fucking to the album, Lou out-dumbed him with: 'I never fuck. I haven't had it up in so long I can't remember when the last time was.'

It all made for a wonderfully delicious piece of rock theatre that would continue to thrill both writers and readers for the rest of Lou Reed's life, but had absolutely nothing to do with music, and everything to do with Lou Reed wanting to stick it to the man. The 'man' in this case being both RCA and Dennis Katz. The idea for *Metal Machine Music*, or at least an album like *MMM*, i.e. one that nobody would be happy with or be able to make money from, stemmed – as far as Lou was concerned it seemed – from Dennis Katz's wholesale rejection of a four-song set of demos Lou had made at Electric Lady studios in January. The irony is these tracks – 'Downtown Dirt', 'Crazy Feeling', 'She's My Best Friend' and the song that was to become the title track of Lou's real next album, 'Coney Island Baby' – were more the kind of things RCA would have been delighted to have released and marketed as the next big-hit Lou Reed album:

raw, stripped-down songs that could be traced straight back to the Velvet Underground's best days. Yet Katz was aghast, not just that 'Downtown Dirt' might be aimed at him. But because he genuinely felt the material was too raw, too angry, not at all what Lou should be doing right now. After he forced Lou to shelve the project, sending him back out on tour instead, the payback, recorded just three months later, would be *Metal Machine Music*.

When RCA suggested releasing the album on their specialist Red Seal imprint – used mainly for classical music records – Lou baulked, insisting *MMM* should be marketed and promoted exactly as any other new album would be. With RCA having no option, contractually, but to comply, when *Metal Machine Music* hit the stores in July 1975 it did so wrapped in a wonderfully black-on-black gatefold sleeve with a supercool shot of Lou bedecked in leathers and shades on its front. Casual browsers, or teenage kids not hip to the brouhaha raging about it in the hip music press, would take *MMM* as the latest offering from the same crazy go-man-go who'd sucker-punched the world with *Sally Can't Dance* and *Transformer*. RCA withdrew the album from circulation after just three weeks, after record shops reported unprec-edented levels of returns from 'dissatisfied customers'. Lou feigned outrage, failing to convince sceptical reporters that he'd directed RCA to put disclaimers on the sleeve, thus: 'Warning: no vocals. Best cut: none. Sounds like: static on a car radio.' They had merely added the printed subtitle: An *Electronic Instrumental Composition*, which as descriptions go ranks alongside characterising a full-scale tsunami as a large moving body of water.

Writing about *Metal Machine Music* in *Creem*, Lester Bangs, contrary to the end, tongue very firmly dandling from his mouth, observed: 'I have heard this record characterized as "anti-human" and "anti-emotional". That it is, in a sense, since it is music made more by tape recorders, amps, speakers, microphones and ring modulators than any set of human hands and emotions. But so what? Almost all music today is anti-emotional and made by machines too. From Elton John to disco... At least Lou is upfront about it.'

Speaking about it in 2003, Reed recalled: 'I hadn't intended it for an audience that didn't want it, but what you're neglecting is that it was taken off the market in less than three weeks. So it didn't get to any audience in particular except as a bootleg. So whoever got it then got it because they wanted it. It didn't infiltrate any kind of audience, any kind of mainstream audience because after three weeks it was gone.'

None of the other reviewers were so charitable: *Rolling Stone* named it Worst Album of the Year. Even long term fans shook their heads and wondered if this time the Phantom of Rock had done more than just fake his own death. Lou revelled in the barbarism, calling *MMM* a 'giant fuck-you' to 'all those fucking assholes' that came to his shows 'and yell for "Vicious" and "Walk On The Wild Side".'

As the years sped by, Lou Reed would try and rationalise this period in his career, seeing it as the inevitable conclusion to a time when he had simply become the victim of his own death-mask persona. 'It was kinda like my own fault, up to a point,' he told Barney Hoskyns in 1996. 'I allowed it, and it was kind of a convenient thing to duck behind and use as a shield against just about everything – the dark prince and all this shit. And it was offered to me; I didn't have to do anything to get it. In the end it was a straitjacket and it was very confining, but... I didn't know any better, I hadn't done this before.' Over time, he developed a new backstory as to how it all came about. Speaking to Ian Fortnam about the genesis of *MMM* in 2003, he explained: 'I was somebody who really liked heavy metal, as it was called back then, electric guitars blowing up amplifiers, and the sound of broken speakers, and I thought it would be a lot of fun not to have to worry about a drum, and not have anything for anybody to sing so you didn't have to worry about a key...'

Back in the late summer of 1975, however, the fallout from *MMM* had left Lou out on his ear. Returning from a tour of Australia and Japan, his relationship with Dennis Katz broken beyond repair, he found himself without management, or the financial safety net that allowed, and with a record company that had no wish to release any more of his music but to whom he still apparently owed up to half a million dollars, he would later claim. Unable to keep up the payments on his apartment and with no money coming into his account while his affairs were being sorted out, Lou Reed threw himself on the mercy of RCA, whom he offered to make a properly commercial record for, and quickly, in return for their renewed support. With the artist over a barrel, which is where record companies always liked them best, RCA agreed to put Lou and Rachel up at a downtown hotel, while he spent ten days in October writing and recording the album that would become *Coney Island Baby*.

Resurrecting all but one of the songs from the Katz-rejected demo of nine months before (the exception being 'Downtown Dirt', the track explicitly about Dennis), Lou proceeded to make his most listener-friendly collection of post-Velvets songs since *Transformer*, though without that totemic album's touches of musical genius from Bowie and Ronson, of course. Aided by a young engineer, Godfrey Diamond, after Steve Katz walked out claiming Lou was 'out of his mind', *Coney Island Baby* would in fact be the first of his albums that Lou Reed would claim his own production credit for. The results were surprisingly listen-able, opening with the playful 'Crazy Feeling', with its light George Harrison guitar, sweet harmonies and corny doorbell dinging over the chorus. Like almost all the songs on the album, 'Crazy Feeling' is clearly about Rachel, the 'queen of the scene'. The light mood continues in almost identikit style through 'Charley's Girl', which was really all about Lou's 'girl', of course. Even the first substantial track on the album, 'She's My Best Friend', ostensibly a retread of an old Velvets number but here repurposed to become an even more direct, almost moving tribute to Rachel, who is 'certainly not your average dog or car'. The track is really brought to life though by the scintillating guitar breaks of both session player and future Kiss and Meat Loaf contributor Bob Kulick and of Lou himself, back playing electric on one of his own records for the first time since *Transformer*. An added veneer that adds hugely to the overall feeling on the album that this might just actually be Lou Reed telling it straight for once.

As if as reward for sitting through these apparently heart-felt songs of love and devotion, albeit shrouded in the usual spells and potions required of all Lou Reed songs, side one of *Coney Island* finished with one of the most powerfully real- ised, subversive and at the time genuinely disturbing tracks since 'Sister Ray', the dark, down-at-heel and dangerous to know 'Kicks'. Built on a snaking guitar rhythm beneath which bustles the snatched conversation of what sounds like a roomful of speed freaks all vying for attention with the most outrageous dawn-patrol anecdote, Lou stabs out the words like the knife the song's protagonist uses to get his 'kicks'. When Lou starts to snarl about killing someone being 'way better than sex now', marvelling when the blood begins to flow that this, surely, is 'the final thing to do now', the revulsion is real, as is the creeping fascination. Like a mouth-baiting first cigarette or the sound of a juddering last breath. It is compelling and insane and oh so yum. 'Kicks' would immediately become one of the highlights of the Lou Reed live show, right up there with 'Heroin' and 'Sweet Jane', for years to come.

Side two of the album is like the sniggering calm after the upsetting storm. Opening with 'A Gift', in a deliberately antagonising Lou Reed classic he assumes the pose of a Mick Jagger, shot through the looking glass: 'I'm just a gift, to the women of this world...' One of the great bad-taste jokes he liked to make, in song and in person, you could call it juvenile or misogynistic and Lou would have taken it as a compliment. Similarly, 'Ooh Baby', about a topless dancer who used to work in a massage parlour and who makes everybody go ooh baby ooh-ooh-ooh. Well, obviously.

The jokes end, though, with the final brace of tracks. 'Nobody's Business', another handholding paean to Rachel in defiance of a world that can't leave them alone even though they will never know or understand what they have, is another track that exemplifies how simple yet wonderfully wrought the playing on the whole album is. So that while *Coney Island Baby* – or any other album Lou Reed would make – could never hope to equal the matchless production of *Transformer*, it contained a warmth and – who woulda thunk it – sincerity that Lou hadn't evinced as a songwriter since he was baring his soul on 'Pale Blue Eyes'. The coup-de-grâce, though, is saved for the very end and the simply beautiful title track, 'Coney Island Baby'. Listening to it for the first time back in 1975, I found myself waiting for the catch, that wink of the over-made-up eye that let you in on the whole sick joke. But it never comes. Not even when Lou camply sings of 'wanting to play football for the coach', which of course he never did. But it's the sensual, half-moon mood this creates – candlelight and Dubonnet on ice, the comedown from the five-day speed bender, an unexpected moment of soul-baring majesty – that sets you up for the breathtakingly emotional denouement, when the guitars explode like dark stars, and Lou sings – really sings at last! – about the 'princess... on the hill, who loved you even though she knew you was wrong...'. Even the last half-heard line where Lou breaks character to address Rachel directly – 'Man, I swear I'd give the whole thing up for you' – was impossible to send up.

Maybe it was the lack of agenda, the simple need to shuddup and pay the bills, but for an album intended as a quickie throwaway, a gift to the record company they could sell like used cars, *Coney Island Baby* was truly exceptional.

What's more, it did its job, returning Lou Reed to the US Top 40, and becoming his first big hit in France, where they understand such things and where Lou Reed would retain folk hero status till the end of his days.

The glowing reviews – in relief as much as anything – that greeted the release of *Coney Island Baby*, in the shops in time for Christmas 1975, reflected this return to form. Writing in *Rolling Stone*, Larry 'Ratso' Sloman, then making a name for himself as the inside guy on Bob Dylan's *Rolling Thunder Revue* tour, described Reed as 'a master narrator, short story writer at heart'. In the *Village Voice*, James Walcott nearly tripped over his own adjectives: '… Evoking Genet decadence… Warhol chic, European ennui…' More down to earth and more to the point, Vivien Goldman's review in *Sounds* complimented the album's 'recitative style, the languorous fall on certain words, the poetic urgency and resonances in certain lines'; adding, pointedly: 'But it's not derivative, because it's solid Lou Reed, unmistakable.'

Lou even got Mick Rock to shoot the cover, a kind of updated *Transformer* in which Lou ditches the leather and shades and reappears in a clingy bodysuit tux and bowtie, his still-white face only semi-obscured this time behind what once would have been described as a raffishly tilted hat.

As 1976 dawned over lower Manhattan, for the first time in years Lou Reed suddenly felt he might just own the future after all. Gone were the managers, mentors and collaborators who had been good while they lasted but ultimately held him back, he decided. Now with a record back in the charts and lucrative tour bookings piling up at his agent's office, Lou Reed was ready to ride into the sun once more.

Top of his list of fresh objectives was a new record deal. Despite the strong sales of *Coney Island Baby*, and irrespective of the long support the label had given through the sales-debacle of *Berlin* and the auto-destruction of *Metal Machine Music*, Lou still resented being put into the position, as he saw it, of having to kowtow to a company that only appreciated his work when it was buzzing around the Top 40. He wasn't just another schmuck pop star, willing to blow anybody that offered to spin his disc on their show, he was an artist; how many times and in how many ways did he have to prove that before anyone at RCA started taking him seriously?

When the legendary music biz mogul Clive Davis phoned him out of the blue one day, Lou was virtually jumping up and down with excitement. 'Do you know who just called!' he cried, taking Rachel in his arms. The former head of Columbia Records, Clive Davis had personally overseen the recording careers in America of Janis Joplin, Santana, Earth, Wind & Fire, Aerosmith, Bruce Springsteen, Billy Joel, and dozens of others. Davis had known Reed for some years, following his career more with curiosity than real interest – too many *snags* as Bowie had once sung – but with Lou's RCA deal at an end yet his career profile higher than ever, and with Clive then launching his own new label, Arista, who had recently signed and had great success with Patti Smith, now seemed the perfect time to be talking to Lou Reed about where he wanted his career to go next.

On this Lou was now perfectly clear. He never wanted to be broke and beholden to anyone again. And for that to happen he needed to sell records. Music to Clive's ears. He immediately sanctioned a five-album deal intended to make Lou Reed into a star of the magnitude of lesser – according to Lou, anyway – but till then much more bankable talents, he had to admit, like Springsteen, like Elton John, like Joni fucking Mitchell and Rod bullshit Stewart. It was the beginning of a great adventure, Lou told Rachel.

   And it so nearly was too.

8
Hey, Shut Up!

The next five years working with Clive Davis and Arista should have been the happiest, most productive years so far of Lou Reed's career. With both men agreeing on a clear goal – to take what these days would be called the Lou Reed brand and extend it to as many hit records as possible – the path ahead was surely ready to be laid with gold and platinum records. Lou was even talking to Rachel about a new kind of domesticity. They would never be 'your average dog or cat' couple, but they did discuss moving from Lou's two-room Upper East Side apartment out to a house in the countryside, and they even bought a dog, two in fact: miniature Dachshunds they called The Baron and The Duke, which they liked to walk in Washington Square Park on Sunday afternoons, usually after coming down from another 48 hour speed bender. Indeed there's a hilarious picture of the two, taken around this time, doing just that, Rachel tottering in leathers and high heels alongside Lou, also in black leather jacket and black jeans, the ubiquitous black shades topped off by a jauntily-angled black leather cap, trying to keep up with The Baron and The Duke.

The first Lou Reed album recorded for Arista was intended to spell out this message loud and clear. Titled *Rock And Roll Heart*, it would contain 12 tracks, eight of which would be less than three minutes long, and only three over four minutes. The studio band would also be stripped back to its simplest, some would say dullest, form, with Lou now playing all the guitars, and stalwart keyboardist Michael Fonfara now assuming direct leadership over the other musicians. Fonfara would later compare the way the music came together as 'like Method acting'. In fact, this was to be Lou-Reed-by-numbers, from the intently staring image of a blue-screened Lou on the cover, to the stately self-regard of the title track, the only song on the album that would survive in the collective memory.

The opening track, 'I Believe In Love', appeared on first listen to set the tone: clearly tongue-in-cheek lyrics, deliberately banal melody, Lou trying to stop himself laughing as he delivers one of his feeblest, most irritating lead vocals... yeah, we get it, white boy, doing it uptown, it's a put-on, right? Just another New York sideswipe at the suckers and A-heads busy making nothing out of something, right?

Maybe. But then 'Banging On My Drum' comes rushing in like it's got something to say, except it hasn't, beyond the obvious ha-ha pun about masturbating. Featuring a two-line lyric, the first of which is just the title repeated 15 times, this was the dumbest Lou Reed track since... well, 'I Believe In Love', two minutes and 12 seconds before. But wait, for there is worse to come. 'Follow The Leader', a bit of cheap ramalama that Lou had been joking around with for years, but which at least features five lines of lyrics, one of which of course is again merely the title sung repeatedly ad nauseam. At which point, the penny drops. This is the summer of 1976 and disco is the new reigning king of New York, and Lou Reed is cleverly cashing in by giving us his own unique version of disco, all squalling saxophones and mulch-keyboards, with the kind of drums that think they're more interesting than anybody else in the room.

'I used to love the guy who played rhythm guitar for James Brown,' Lou would later tell Bruce Pollock. 'What he's doing is the pure rhythmic chords without all that garbage.' That 'garbage' being anyone that might try and bring some sense to what Reed was now doing with his monkey-see, monkey-do music. So-called real musicians and critics, 'They seem to think… that I can't possibly mean what I say.' The actuality was that he *did* mean it.

Even 'You Wear It So Well', with its portentous piano intro, forgoes lyrics of any merit in favour of thought-bubble repetition and droning pointless backing vocals. When Lou Reed later boasted that he had written all the lyrics at the mixing stage of the recording, no one batted an eye. The only surprise was that he actually needed to write them down. That he wasn't just speed-burbling to himself whenever they put a vocal mike in front of him. Most excruciating, though, are those few tracks where Reed attempts – and fails miserably – to actually write a coherent verse or two, like on the abysmally dull 'Ladies Pay' or the impossibly naff 'Senselessly Cruel', like Springsteen on downers. At least the equally empty 'Chooser Or The Chosen One' dispenses with lyrics, allowing us to bathe in its inert simplicity. Or not, as the case would increasingly come to be, over the course of not too many listens.

Only the title track – on any other album a fairly standard Lou-Reed-doing-Lou-Reed castoff, but set in this context the only jewel in an otherwise pathetically cardboard crown – marries a decent tune to some perfectly acceptable lyrics, and becomes the mantra for the whole sorry enterprise, a kind of tribute to personal freedom as defined by gross stupidity and emotional lumpishness. To wit: 'I guess I'm just dumb, cos I know that I ain't smart. But deep down inside, I got a rock'n'roll heart.'

Fair enough then, you don't feel like saying.

'I think I've kept out of the way on this album more successfully than ever before,' he announced, with an apparently straight face in one of the interviews to promote the album when it was released in October 1976. 'I always look so crazy and disorganised but I'm not.'

Clive Davis was especially disappointed. He knew the *Rock And Roll Heart* album was a mishmash of New York street slang and sluggish late-night TV-dinner soundtracks, but in the title track he discerned at least the makings of a hit, telling Lou he would make him a million dollars if he'd just consent to allowing Clive to take the track back into the studio and add some magic-number touches of his own. Perhaps needing something, or someone, to kick against, and despite his craven need for cash, Lou fought Clive every step of the way. The track was just fine as it was, thank you. I'm an artist, man! I thought you got that? Davis could only shrug and walk away. But he began to understand better now what RCA had been up against all those years.

In fact, very few people were getting Lou Reed any more, outside his coterie of diehard fans and a handful of bottom-feeding critics whose own ambitions now lay in getting as wasted as they fondly imagined Lou Reed to always be. And even they ran for cover when *Rock And Roll Heart* landed like a dog turd on their desks. Nick Kent in the *NME* said what everyone else was thinking when he wrote: 'Certainly don't bother with this record.' It was good advice most people followed, and *Rock And Roll Heart* became Lou's biggest flop in America since *Berlin* (not counting *MMM*, which arrived stillborn) and didn't even make the Top 100 in Britain. Even France ignored it.

Clive Davis, meanwhile, who'd been round the block so many times they would one day name it after him, decided to play the long game. He'd seen Lou Reed records fail before, usually right before Lou pulled a rabbit out of a hat and had the biggest hit of his career. He gambled on the future, directing Arista to bankroll a world tour, as well as a futuristic stage set that comprised 48 flickering video TV screens, all with his image on, à la album cover, their blue lights throwing the stage into a deep azure haze. The most lavish show he had undertaken, unlike the speed-cracked *Rock'n'Roll Animal* and *Sally Can't Dance* tours, which sometimes barely stretched to 90 minutes, the all-new *Rock And Roll Heart* revue would feature 21 songs and last for two and a half hours, and would include all but four of the tracks from *Rock And Roll Heart*, which caused some consternation among the more discerning of Reed's audiences – reports came back of teenagers staring as blankly at the stage as the TV sets staring unblinking back out at them – but when they worked acted as punctuation marks for the grander, more readily applauded set pieces like

'I'm Waiting For The Man', 'Walk On The Wild Side' and the encore each night, 'White Light/White Heat'. The live band, still led by Michael Fonfara, also featured a surprise new recruit in Ornette Coleman's trumpeter Don Cherry. Suddenly, Lou had to up his game. Gone was the frazzled walking skeleton with pale yellow skin whose fingers were so stiff from all the drugs he could no longer barely hold the mike let alone play the guitar of more recent tours, and in his place came a guy whose hair was now back to its natural dark colour and who pulled on a guitar like he actually knew what to do with it. He was also singing better than he had for years. Like, hey, man, a cat like Don Cherry ain't gonna put up with no fag junkie shit, better getcha ass up there and wail, bro. Which, pleasingly, is exactly what Lou Reed now did.

When Caroline Coon caught up with the tour in Los Angeles, she wrote a fascinating report for *Melody Maker*, in which she described hanging out with Lou and Rachel, and really getting a feel for what life on the road was like for the two of them together. After a disastrous tour of New Zealand the previous year, when Lou missed Rachel so much he would go to sleep at night still on the phone to her in New York, staying on the line so that he could continue talking to her as soon as he opened his eyes, before eventually finding an excuse to simply leave the tour and run home to her, Rachel was now Lou's constant companion on the road, too.

'I never said I was tasteful. I'm not tasteful.'

Concerned for her health, Lou asks Caroline to feel Rachel's forehead to try and gauge her temperature. Then chastises her: 'How is it that *I'm* the voice of reason? It's me who tells you to put your coat on and it's you who should be looking after *me*. We'll end up this tour hating each other!'

'No, we won't,' said Rachel.

Lou then describes their new life of mostly staying home and playing with his 'toys', his guitars and video games and cassette recorders. 'I guess it's something to do if you've never done it,' he says as Rachel looks on saying nothing.

When Coon asks whether he is rich now he tells her truthfully, 'I made a lot of money... There are lawsuits over that', referring to the suit and countersuit he was tussling over with Dennis and Steve Katz.

This remarkable journalist also gets an astonishing admission from him about *Metal Machine Music*. 'No matter what you say about me, that was commercial suicide. It was calculated – on purpose with no "ifs" and "buts". The critics tried to rationalise it by saying I was afraid of stardom. Ha! Yeh? Okay. Take it any way you want.' He was now in full rant mode: 'I made that double-album because that's what I wanted to do and that's what it was. And I happen to like the record, so there! And I like *Coney Island Baby* and *Rock And Roll Heart*, so there. There!' He also rhapsodised about his new deal with Arista and the man who had made it all possible, his new father figure, Clive Davis. 'I got lucky and met Clive. And now I've got my way – top to bottom control all the way. Now I'm out there with guys who are playing my way. It's no back-up band. We've been playing together a long time, but it's *my* band. And it's real.'

It made a nice change, he suggested, from the days when only Keith Richards would beat him in the annual music polls category 'Which Rock Star Is Most Likely To Die', acknowledging: 'Most of the audience were showing up to see if "He" would drop dead three-quarters through the show! Well, that's what was going on. I knew that. And if that's how they wanted me to go then that's how they were going to get me.'

There was also, at the time of the *Rock And Roll Heart* world tour, another development in the world of rock which, yet again, lifted Lou Reed out of the quagmire of his wilfully topsy-turvy solo career and back squarely in the critical spotlight. Suddenly, with the advent in Britain of bands like the Sex Pistols, The Clash and The Damned, and their counterparts in America, specifically New York, where a whole next generation of club bands were emerging all at the same time, including names like Television, The Ramones, and Richard Hell and the Voidoids, Lou Reed, once the Godfather of Glam, was about to be transformed into the High Priest of Punk, becoming one of the few 1970s artists – along with Iggy Pop, David Bowie and Patti Smith – that punk did not lay to waste with their ground zero approach to the musical past.

John Cale may have looked with disdain at the posthumous plaudits the Velvet Underground now received from their young punk peers like garlands of thorns, laughing off any suggestion that Lou Reed had anything to do with this new so-called movement, hissing: 'Lou has his whole life sorted out now. He's become the Jewish businessman we always knew he was.'

Lou, though, was happy to lap up this newfound adulation, checking out the new wave of bands then playing CBGBs on the Bowery, talking trash to the kids from the new fanzine *Punk*, getting off on seeing how much they were getting off on the fact *he* was actually *talking* to *them*. By the time he came to record his next album, Lou Reed knew exactly what kind of record he needed to do. All he lacked, though he was loath to admit it at the time, was the physical and mental stamina to pull it off. The speed, once his most powerful creative tool, was now having diminishing returns on his songwriting prowess, and no matter how much meth Lou shot into his body or how many nights he fidgeted in his apartment with his cassette recorders and guitars, as Rachel looked on bored, unmoved by the punk movement that seemed to merely ape what Lou had been doing for years, only in much more earnest, far less far-out and fun ways, Lou really could not get it up to write and record enough new songs for what he knew in his brittle bones would be an important album for him. There could be no cruising with this, no lounge act snapping its fingers, playing the jazz-junk-disco card, this one would have to deliver on what the new punk audience saw as Reed's real legacy, what all these new young cats like Tom Verlaine and Richard Hell and Joey Ramone were more than ready to do in his place if he didn't get ready. Now.

The result was *Street Hassle*, an album that contained some of his most audacious work for years, yet also crawled with clangers, a gun that fired only blanks at least half the time. An album that he couldn't even get together to record in one piece, somehow talking Clive Davis into letting him record most of the tracks live onstage, because it was more punk, he seemed to argue, when in reality because it was just more easy. Lou was talking fast again. This had better be good.

It was. And even when it wasn't it was still better than *Rock And Roll Heart*, which wasn't much but just enough. At first, though, it looked like another bummer shimmying down the road, its cringe-inducing opener, 'Gimme Some Good Times', a typical Lou Reed joke you had heard far too many times already. Its jive-ass intro, laid over the live backing track recorded on his last German tour, both parodying the received wisdom of who Lou Reed was supposed to be, in the punk era, and inadvertently sending up the idea that he might still somehow be relevant in the new rock reality. The next track, though, 'Dirt', was the real thing, whatever year you happened to be thinking about when you heard it for the first time. Seemingly a more savage update on the rejected *Coney Island Baby* track 'Downtown Dirt', again the backing track is recorded live, but Lou's venomous diatribe is clearly a studio take, so clearly does he sound out lines like 'They'd eat shit and say it tasted good, if there was some money in it for them.'

It's only its authentic nastiness, though, that finally resonates. For the real reborn Lou Reed, the one who now reached for punk transcendence, you had to wait for the delirious title track, an 11-minute opus divided into three musical sections, like the true street opera that it was: 'Waltzing Matilda', 'Street Hassle' and 'Slip Away', the latter featuring an uncredited Bruce Springsteen on backing vocals. This was *Berlin* all over again, but set much closer to home in New York, and not stretched across an album but condensed into a both-ends-burning short that stings the mind's eye.

'It's a great monologue,' is how Lou would describe it years later. 'But there's two monologues going on really.

There's the person in part one, the person in part two and these two couldn't be more polar opposite. The person acting out the first part is one way, and the complete opposite person is on the other side in part two. They're not even vaguely of the same species.'

The cinematic 'Waltzing Matilda', introduced by a scraping cello that sounds like the mating call of an ambulance on its way to an emergency, opens on a scene of a wealthy woman client picking up a male prostitute, a street corner transaction that turns into something surprisingly tender, so that when the boy leaves the next morning 'neither one regretted a thing'. The next section, 'Street Hassle', takes place elsewhere on the same metaphorical street and concerns another kind of transaction, this one though gone horribly wrong. 'Hey, that cunt's not breathing,' sings the narrator, a drug dealer gazing at the inert overdosed form of the girlfriend of one of his clients. Advising him to 'grab your old lady by the feet' out onto the street where by morning, she'll be 'just another hit and run'. The concluding part three, 'Slip Away', concerns love and death and what some people might think it all means and features a brilliantly evocative spoken-word recital of the first verse by Bruce Springsteen – uncredited because of his own legal 'hassles' at the time with his record label – who concludes, poignantly, with the line: 'Tramps like us, we were born to pay...'

Years later, on his 2004 live album *Animal Serenade*, on which he performs a truncated but no less powerful version of 'Street Hassle', Lou Reed wrote in the liner notes of how he wanted to write a great monologue set to rock, something that could have been written by William Burroughs, Hubert

Selby, John Rechy, Tennessee Williams, Nelson Algren, or even Raymond Chandler. 'You mix it all up and you have 'Street Hassle',' he wrote.

It's a highlight the rest of the album then has to climb down from, but it's worth the exhaustion. Three of the five tracks on side two were pulled from the back pocket of a pair of old jeans: 'Real Good Time Together' was a Velvets live staple in 1969 but had recently been co-opted as the opener of Patti Smith's live show; 'Leave Me Alone' was another *Coney Island Baby* reject; and the Lenny Bruce-esque 'I Wanna Be Black', the second most talked-about track on the album after the title track, was originally written for *Sally Can't Dance*, but rejected by nervous RCA executives who really didn't, uh, get it. With its mocking lines about wanting to be black 'and shoot 20 feet of jism', or be 'like Martin Luther King and get myself shot in the spring', oh, and 'have a big prick too', it would be years, in fact, before anyone would allow Reed to get away with releasing it. But the story of the song had become a music paper legend, bootlegs of Lou performing it live had come out, and Lou never stopped talking about it in interviews, going so far as to claim in the run-up to recording *Street Hassle* that he was going to make 'I Wanna Be Black' the title track of his next album, and that the cover would feature a picture of Lou in blackface eating a watermelon. In the end the only way to stem the 'controversy' was to just release the damn song, so that everyone could get over it, see it for what it was: a cheap-shot semi-comic musical folly. Bad, Lou...

That left just 'Shooting Star', throwaway nonsense about a 'Cadillac metal car' that grates, and the album closer, 'Wait', a just half-successful attempt at what can only be described as a pop song, replete with sugared backing vocals and irritating keyboard and sax motif that thankfully runs out of steam before anyone can really notice.

Clive Davis, more pleased, if still uncertain, about the patchy *Street Hassle* than the abysmal *Rock And Roll Heart*, still found himself being dragged into studio squabbles throughout. When Lou, somewhat astonishingly, invited Richard Robinson back into the fold to co-produce the sessions with him, Clive saw it as a positive sign that this wasn't going to be another navel-gazer. When Robinson then walked out after one poisoned barb too many from Lou, and Lou announced he would completely produce the album himself, Clive began to worry. Then, unable to sway Lou about turning the end section of the title track into a longer piece that Clive thought he could turn into a hit single, the Arista chief threw up his hands. Then had to suffer the twin mysteries of Lou both thanking and insulting him in subsequent press interviews about the album. 'When Clive heard the original [title track] he said that it was great, and I should make it longer,' Lou told one interviewer gleefully. 'So I did.' Some time later, however, Lou told someone else: 'Clive Davis came in and told me I should make a new record and throw this one away… The head of Arista is stupid.'

But it was the head of Arista who was still Lou Reed's single biggest supporter, financially, whom the singer was now pushing to his limits. For although *Street Hassle* went some way to restoring his critical reputation, it was an even worse seller than *Rock And Roll Heart*, limping to No. 89 in America and nowhere at all in Britain. Surveying what he was increasingly coming to see as the wreckage of his life and career, in the summer of 1978 Lou Reed, now 36, began to make significant changes to both. Away from the music press microscope, he'd continued to write and publish poetry, though he rarely discussed this in public. He had in fact recently completed a book of poetry, to be called *All The Pretty People*, which he intended to publish that year (though, in the event, he dithered until publication had to be put back indefinitely). When it was announced that he had been awarded a prize as one of the year's best new poets by the obscure but influential American Literary Council of Little Magazines, he aw-shucked about it to friends but kept the news away from the music press. It was the same when he had one of his sketches printed in the highly regarded magazine *Art Direction*. It was cool, sure, but nobody was to know, okay?

Now living with Rachel in a six-room apartment above a bagel shop in Christopher Street, the heart of the gay scene in the West Village, he now decided he'd had enough of dodging bullets, real and figurative. He'd had enough of fights. 'I only have to walk out of my door and I start a fight,' he complained. Of course, he and Rachel had been talking about moving out of the city for a while. Now, though, Lou finally took the plunge, purchasing a sizeable lakeside property in Blairstown, New Jersey, where he would – hold on to yourself – go fishing, breathe fresh air, indulge his new fad – a strictly drug-free fruit juice and nuts diet – and actually have a chance to catch up on some of the years of sleep he'd missed. 'It smells great,' he told *Creem*. 'Even if you wanted to do something there's nothing there.'

Using it at first as a weekend retreat, Lou began to want to spend more and more time outside the city he had spent a lifetime writing about. However, Rachel, a born city freak, was less enamoured of the countryside life and suddenly it was okay for Lou to be apart from her for days at a time. Lou would never leave New York for long. Like Rachel, he was as much a part of the city as its fire hydrants and sewers. But he was now approaching 40 and his lifestyle choices were adjusting accordingly. Suddenly Rachel, a living symbol of the life he was now shedding like a wretched old skin, was losing her allure for Lou. The feeling was mutual. By year's end, after one mini-breakup and one lengthy trial separation, the relationship was finally over and Lou told her she should find her own place to live. Once she'd gone, it was like she'd never even existed. Although he never shut her completely out of his heart, continuing to recall her fondly among friends, he never spoke of her publicly again.

Before that, though, as if to bid that time in his life one final adieu, Lou Reed released the stupendous *Live: Take No Prisoners*. One of the greatest, most brutally honest and fantastically funny live rock albums ever released.

Recorded at two shows at New York's Bottom Line club in May 1978, and featuring a superbly splenetic Lou Reed in absolutely blistering form, *Take No Prisoners* was the live summation of everything the post-Velvets Lou Reed had been and become over the past near-decade. Beginning on a suitably heightened note with the sound of a matchbook being struck, a cigarette being lit and inhaled, followed by Lou, his lip audibly curling: 'Hello. Sorry we were late but we were just tuning...' A tape then audibly begins to roll and we find ourselves at the start of the show, the small but vociferous crowd whooping and yelling out his name, as the band did indeed tune up, before Lou strolls up to the mike and snarls: 'Whatsamatter, we keep you *waitin'* or somethin'? Are we *late?*', followed by more crowd baiting, Lou quoting Yeats: 'The best lack all conviction while the worst are filled with a passion and intensity. Now you figure out where I am.' Before the band comes absolutely smashing into the riff of 'Sweet Jane', which then goes on for over eight minutes as Lou digresses again and again into the kind of backstories and side bars that future MTV-style story-behind-the-song programmes could never hope to match, including how much Lou hates 'fucking Barbra Streisand' for thanking 'all the little people' in her Academy Award acceptance speeches. 'Fuck short people and tall people, man. I like middle people. People from Wyoming.'

From there the album takes off like a giddy vulture into something that is part rock'n'roll – the band, led as always by Michael Fonfara, is *hot* tonight – part Lenny Bruce comedy act, part confessional, part pure confrontation. '*Hey, shut up!*' when someone interrupts his flow. 'Are you fucking *deaf?*' at another juncture to someone brave enough to risk a verbal exchange. A weird otherworldly musical milieu where 'I Wanna Be Black', with its extra, improvised asides, is suddenly hilarious and self-mocking. 'Let's ask the chicks…' Where 'Satellite Of Love' and 'Pale Blue Eyes' are equal parts soulful and wincingly revealing, and, somewhat shockingly in this context, played virtually straight. 'So now everybody's gonna say Lou Reed's mellowed, he's older. He didn't act mean he talked. Oh boy. I say we'll mug you later, all right? You feel better?' Of these relatively straightforwardly rendered songs, though, 'Coney Island Baby' is the best. Still jammed with dark side trips – 'I was more of a pole vaulter' he jokes of the lines about wanting to play football for the coach. Yet although you don't hear it on *Take No Prisoners*, he would routinely begin the song at these shows with the words: 'This is for Lou and Rachel.'

'Street Hassle' begins with an aside about how *Metal Machine Music* 'was born', as Lou fiddles with a feedbacking microphone, before he descends deep into character, playing each part in a different crazily garbled voice, including that of a snide, know-all narrator, as the two female backing singers, Angel Howell and Chrissy Faith – one black, one white – add a lush, breathless gloss to the street slime Lou is smearing the stage so painstakingly with. Most wondrously of all though is 'Walk On The Wild Side', which follows, and goes on for 17 minutes without ever quite getting to the song, the 'coloured girls' coming in just once, and then only for a moment before Lou interrupts them to return to his speed-jive account of how he came to write the song in the first place, replete with all the biographical details of a book, from the Broadway producers who talked him into writing a song with that title, to how he was working as a typist at the time, to who the real people were he eventually named in the later version, and, ultimately, and most startlingly, what it all probably meant. Probably. Along the way we are treated to some more classic asides: 'I do Lou Reed better than anybody else, so I thought I'd get in on it,' he announces to braying laughter. 'Hey, watch me turn into Lou Reed!' He also takes the opportunity to mock his critics, raging at Robert Christgau, calling him 'a toe fucker' for his pathetic A, B, C ratings system, telling on John Rockwell of the *New York Times*, who 'comes to CBGBs with a bodyguard'.

'That's what *Take No Prisoners* was about,' Lou would later tell Sandy Robertson. 'Because everybody said I never talk. I was in my hometown of New York, so I talked... I thought of even titling it *Lou Reed Talks, And Talks, And Talks...* but we called it *Take No Prisoners* because we were doing a job... All of a sudden this drunk guy sitting alone at the front shouts, "Lou! Man! Take no prisoners, Lou!" And then he took his head and smashed it as hard as he could to the drumbeat. We saw him doing it and we were taking bets that that man would not move again. But he got up and bam, bam! On the table! And that was only halfway through!'

Yet at another, telling juncture on the album, Lou dry-quips: 'Misrepresentation's not my game.' And it becomes clear he's not really joking at all. Never has been, perhaps. Least of all whenever we thought we heard the laughter in his songs.

Amazingly, Clive Davis, who had tussled with Lou about his previous albums, trying to squeeze a hit single out of them, to no avail, now looked on benignly at this latest turn in events. Or at least, that was how Lou Reed liked to remember it a quarter of a century later.

'Clive Davis was always very supportive of me, when I first played him the *Street Hassle* album, first it's 'I Wanna Be Black' and then into 'Street Hassle' [and] you hear "that cunt's not breathing" and I said "Clive?" And he said, "You are what you are. I knew that when I got you". And with *Take No Prisoners* it was more of the same. I wasn't a surprise to Clive, he didn't go "He did what?" He knew what I was. That's why he signed me. He didn't object to that. He knew what he was getting, he knew I did things like that. Clive's smart.'

Of course, Lou would have his rationale behind *Take No Prisoners* – and no matter how implausible it sounded at the time, it turned out to be (mostly) true. From now on there would be 'no more bullshit, no more dyed hair, faggot junkie trip[s].' He now claimed he'd been merely playing a part, just like all the other fake Lou Reeds now out there. 'I can play him well – really well,' he said.

Though not for much longer...

9
The New Mask

They say the darkest hour is right before the dawn. Yet Lou Reed's career had suffered so many dark hours, so many false dawns, that by the end of the 1970s the story was simply no longer interesting. The extraordinary generation of artists that had plundered his musical landscape since 1976 – from the Sex Pistols and The Ramones to Joy Division and Talking Heads, and many thousands of different and rarely less than fascinating points between – had left whatever music Lou Reed still felt capable of making little more than a sideshow. A curiosity, at best; the critics more interested in the succession of resurrected old Velvet Underground live tapes and previously unreleased recordings that had begun appearing; those remaining fans that still checked in with his latest work still hoping for the best while expecting only the worst.

In a career built on irony, paradox, miscues and self-harm, it was only fitting perhaps that the last two albums of his Arista deal would be his most concerted efforts to produce new material of a genuinely high standard, which both pleased an audience and spoke more truly of his own art, since the last days of the Velvet Underground: *The Bells* in 1979, a disjointed jazz-rock mix of songs co-written with outsiders like Nils Lofgren and Don Cherry, or with members of his touring band; and *Growing Up In Public* in 1980, an open-hearted if musically underwhelming collaboration with Michael Fonfara.

'My expectations are very high,' he announced in *Creem*. 'I want to do that rock'n'roll thing that's on a level with *The Brothers Karamazov*. I'm starting to build up a body of work. I'm on the right track. I think I haven't done badly. But I think I really haven't scratched the surface. I think I'm just starting.'

But by then it was too late. And hadn't we heard it all before anyway? And so, despite encouraging notices from the critics – old foes like Lester Bangs in *Rolling Stone* acclaimed *The Bells* as 'the only true jazz-rock fusion anybody's come up with since Miles Davis's *On The Corner*'; Robert Christgau in the *Village Voice* described *Growing Up In Public* as an 'unabashedly literate album' – neither album was a hit, each selling less than the one before, becoming the first Lou Reed albums not to even reach the *Billboard* Hot 100.

Describing The Bells as 'a drama', years later Reed would find a whole new context for this work. The album had been 'constructed in the studio and sung one time and one time only, I'm making those lyrics up on the spot. And it's an amazing lyric. Whatever it is. I've looked back at that lyric trying to understand it, since it's coming from a different place than usual. Unfettered by anything it's just going free and there it was. Kind of amazing, to go back later to Poe and 'The Bells' and there's my bells. 'And the actresses relate to the actor who comes home late'. Wow, this is my kind of… It's like, 'The Sweet Smell Of Success' and 'This Is My Kind Of Town'. That's my kind of lyric. You just don't know where it's going to go.'

Even touring, for so long a sanctuary of both instant gratification from his audience and instant pay-off from ticket and merchandising revenue, now became drawn-out and obstacle-strewn. At a show in Germany on *The Bells* tour, before several thousand drunken American GIs and pumped-up punks hoping for a rerun of the riotous *Take No Prisoners* album, Lou walked off three times after being shut out by the screams of abuse. When a drunken girl fan jumped onstage and ran at him he panicked and dragged her kicking to the wings where his roadies held her down. When he then ordered his band off the stage, refusing to finish the show, the place rioted and nearly $20,000 worth of damage was done to the venue. To add insult to injury, after the show Lou was arrested by police for bodily assault, and thrown in jail overnight where they took blood and urine samples, to see what he was high on. 'How would you like to get into a [police] van with twelve goose steppers saying they're going to test your blood?' he moaned afterwards. Fortunately, the police found no trace of illegal drugs in his system. A remarkable fact on its own.

Further ignominy was to follow, however, when the tour came to its stop at the Hammersmith Odeon in London, in April. Even more on edge than usual when David Bowie turned up backstage before the show, Lou insisted on the venue keeping all the house lights on during the performance. By now he had rearranged 'Heroin' as a full-on, tub-thumping soul ballad; sang 'Perfect Day' in a weird, strangled falsetto; and insisted the bassist, Ellard Boles, who had co-written some of the material on *The Bells*, sing the first encore, a slow, bruising version of The Supremes' 'You Keep Me Hanging On', while he watched from the wings.

Afterwards, though, Bowie was effusive in his praise and a relieved Lou invited him to dinner at the Chelsea Rendezvous restaurant, along with the rest of the band and their various entourages. The dinner began in a joyful spirit, the two stars offering each other elaborate toasts across the table. Then, as one eyewitness, the legendary *Sounds* writer Giovanni Dadomo, later told me: 'All hell broke loose. Lou suddenly leapt up and threw himself at Bowie, hitting him, really punching him, shouting, "Don't you ever say that to me!" Nobody could believe what they were seeing. Then one of Lou's roadies or bodyguards grabbed him and pulled him off Bowie, and everyone tried to calm things down. Then something happened, Bowie must have said something else, cos Lou grabbed him again by the shirt and whacked him. Hard. He was yelling at him, "I told you never to say that!"'

There was no way back from that and Lou stormed out of the restaurant, followed sheepishly by his band and entourage. A shocked Bowie gathered himself and followed them out too, turning over tables as he went and smashing every single pot plant that lined the way to the exit. The next morning all Lou's appointments, including several scheduled press interviews, were cancelled as it was announced that Reed had already left for the airport.

Back home in New York, when pressed for the reasons behind the outburst, and whether it was true he had actually hit David Bowie, an unrepentant Lou snapped: 'Yes, I hit him – more than once. It was a private dispute.' He refused, though, to say what exactly it was over, adding only: 'It had nothing to do with sex, politics or rock'n'roll.' That he had 'a New York code of ethics'. He scowled. 'In other words, watch your mouth.' Word eventually crept out though that the basis of Lou's rage was in David's response to Lou's only-half-joking inquiry about whether he would like to produce Lou's next album. When Bowie answered in the affirmative, but only on condition that Lou 'clean up his act first', Lou went insane.

Reed's anger bubbled uncomfortably close to the surface again with his next two shows, this time at the Bottom Line in New York, where he chastised the audience for calling out for 'Heroin' – something that had happened at every show Lou had done for the past five years. 'When I say it's my wife and it's my life do you think I'm kidding?' he railed at them. Things went from bad to worse when he spotted Clive Davis sitting near the front in the audience. Looking dead at Clive from the stage, he growled: 'This is for you, Clive.' Then gave him the finger. Before going on: 'Where's the money, Clive? How come I don't hear my album on the radio?' Clive didn't flinch. When a few days later his office issued a press statement from Lou, it read, in part: 'I've always loved Clive, and he happens to be one of my best friends... Trying to read anything deeper into all this is all pointless.'

In truth, however, the working relationship with Clive Davis had been holed beneath the waterline long before that. When his final album for Arista, the unfairly if understandably neglected *Growing Up In Public*, came out in 1980, it was hard to tell any more who cared less, Lou or Clive. Or the fans.

But if his professional career was now off the rails, and he was out of his deal and out of luck with his own audience, Lou Reed's personal life was about to take a significant turn for the better. When, one night at a gay S&M club in the Village called Eulenspiegel, Lou was introduced to Anya Phillips, a Chinese-American entrepreneur best known at that time for her skintight rubber catsuits, at first he was taken aback. Women were not usually welcome at the Eulenspiegel but Anya didn't seem to care and he became impressed by her upfront personality. He was even more taken, however, with the girlfriend Anya introduced him to: a striking, British-born Latin-American artist and designer named Sylvia Morales. By the end of the night, he had got her phone number and arranged to see her again. When a couple of days later Lou did call, Sylvia was surprised and delighted. Perhaps all the terrible things she'd read and heard about this guy weren't so true after all?

Or perhaps Lou Reed, as he put it, 'just didn't want to be that guy any more'. As he would confess years later, in an interview with the great *LA Times* music critic, Robert Hilburn, looking back at that transitional period in his life, at first it was 'a devastating feeling' trying to come to terms with a life without drugs. 'You start thinking what is it that you can do [instead] to, like, hot-rod your writing... You medicate yourself so you can create.' By the end of the 1970s, however, 'I found it to be just the opposite effect. All that just makes it worse.'

At first, friends cooed at this latest development in the love life of the man who just a few short months before had been quoted in *Creem* as saying: 'A woman can get turned off if you're appreciative of her, when what she really wants is to be smacked across the mouth.' But soon Lou and Sylvia were such a regular item that when he announced they were to be married, on 14 February 1980 – Valentine's Day, the old smoothie – they didn't even bother to feign surprise. The change in Lou's personality had been dramatic since the two had met. Already heading for the other side of the rainbow when it came to drugs anyway, now in the wake of his marriage to Sylvia, Lou swore off them completely. He still had an occasional drink – wine with a meal, or on special occasions – but Lou Reed now preferred a burger and a Coke, and a ride on his motorcycle through the New Jersey countryside, to the spectral horrors of intravenous drug use, the very thought of shooting methedrine into his body enough to make him mentally shudder.

The wedding took place at Lou's Christopher Street apartment. A civil ceremony in which Lou had written his own vows, and in which he quoted from two of Delmore Schwartz's poems, similar to his previous marriage to Bettye, this one came at a time when Lou Reed was seeking to withdraw from the squalid mess he had made of so much of his life and career in the 1970s. Unlike the marriage to Bettye, however, this time around Lou was no longer financially desperate, or running to catch up on a career he feared had left him for dead. Nor was this to be the kind of claustrophobically close relationship he had enjoyed with Rachel. Sylvia would occasionally accompany her new husband on his tours, but mainly her role would be as the traditional homemaker.

As Lou told one reporter a couple of months after the wedding: 'I now know that certain things will get taken care of and looked out for on the home front... I've found my flower, so it makes me feel more like a knight.'

There was a temptation for those that had followed his career for longer than 15 minutes to treat such quotes as the further stoned ramblings of an arch-deceiver and self-flagellant. But this time it seemed Lou actually meant it. His 1980 world tour in support of the workmanlike *Growing Up In Public* was declared a drug-free zone, on punishment of being fired from the tour. And in 1981, Lou quit drinking too, and began attending Alcoholics Anonymous sessions in New York. There would be the inevitable fall from the wagon, but never very far or for very long. As long as Sylvia was there to support, Lou was now on the straight and narrow. About as far away from the misadventures of old semi-autobiographical characters like Jim and Caroline as it seemed possible to be.

Equally unexpected came the news, at the end of 1981, that Lou had signed a new record deal – with RCA! There were no fears of another *Metal Machine Music* though, as Reed embarked on a rebirth of his music that would continue, in occasionally zigzagging form, throughout the rest of his life. After years of fighting with former managers, former label executives, former friends and selves, Lou was finally taking care of business. For years, 'I had some very bad people around me, and like a lot of musicians I didn't pay attention to that side of it. Although on the other hand it's quite possible that I wouldn't be here if it wasn't for that. It was pretty terrible – lawsuits for 12 years, some pretty astonishing shit. It's a very dirty business, make no mistake about it.'

When Sylvia took Lou along to see her friend Robert Quine, formerly guitarist with Richard Hell's band the Voidoids, at CBGBs one night, Lou had been tremendously impressed. When Sylvia introduced them afterwards, Lou was astonished when Robert reminded him that they had first met years before, after a Velvet Underground show in San Francisco in 1969.

'I got to know Lou, and the band, then,' Quine would later recall in *ZigZag* magazine. 'They didn't have a lot of fans in San Francisco and when they saw me there every night they became friendly, got me into the club for free, bought me drinks and let me hang around backstage I taped around fifteen or sixteen of those concerts and I still have them lying around somewhere. After that I didn't see Lou for many years. I knew his wife [Sylvia] though, she was a big Voidoids fan.'

Recalling their reconnection that night at CBGBs a decade later he said: 'Afterwards [Lou] grabbed me backstage and raved about my playing. He didn't remember me from San Francisco but it was still very flattering.' When Lou began jamming with Robert at home, it sparked the series of remarkable songs that would become the album that reintroduced Lou Reed to the real world, *The Blue Mask*, which Quine would play on. 'In 1981 he called me up and we did *The Blue Mask*, a record that I'm particularly proud of. We had never played together before going into the studio. There were no rehearsals and most of it was done in one or two takes. I like all the things that I've done with Lou but that will always be special for me.'

Released on RCA in 1982, *The Blue Mask* was a fresh, clear-eyed collection of songs that now ranks in the upper echelon of Lou Reed's greatest works. At the time it came out, though, it faced an uphill task with the critics. Numbed by his recent albums, which neither attained the haphazard heights of *Street Hassle* or *Take No Prisoners*, nor sank to the swampy depths of *Metal Machine Music* or *Sally Can't Dance*, and the 1960s and 1970s now feeling like a faraway world bombed out of existence by the punk apocalypse, mainly critics found the new album mystifying.

Not that Lou was, of course, interested in making things easy for them. That said, it was impossible not to be immediately knocked out by the sound on *The Blue Mask*. After years of jazz-rock flirtations, disco pastiches, strange cocktail ballads, trad-rock for mustachioed musos, leg-sawing orchestras and, going all the way back to the Bowie days, that strangely amputated form of glam rock, for Lou Reed to come out with a musical statement as direct as he did on the ten blood-purifying tracks on *The Blue Mask* was so unexpected it was almost impossible to take in the first half-dozen times you navigated your way, mouth agape, around its grooves.

It soon became clear that Reed had assembled his best band possibly ever. It wasn't just the addition of the superbly simpatico Quine, whose guitar twines itself around Lou's own chiming echoes like a benevolent parasite; it was the shrewd decision to hire the bassist Fernando Saunders, whose experience moulding the rhythms of jazz-rock giants like Jan Hammer, John McLaughlin and Jeff Beck into warm fuzzy new parameters adds a wonderful heat to the sound; and the drummer Doane Perry, who could play jazz, rock, classical, folk or anything else you cared to name in any combination you liked, fitted like a glove. It was as though the Velvet Underground had re-emerged from a time capsule with a weird new ability to actually play their instruments properly, minus the extra cheese most 'proper' musicians insisted on.

The same year Lou Reed began jamming with Robert Quine and writing the songs for *The Blue Mask*, John Cale was telling the *NME* he wished Lou Reed 'would stop writing the same song'. Now finally he was ready to do just that. Opening with the spellbinding 'My House', on the surface a hymn to his and Sylvia's new life at the farmhouse in New Jersey, underneath a startling evocation of his old friend and 'the first great man I ever met', Delmore Schwartz. 'My Dedalus to your Bloom,' he almost weeps, 'Was such a perfect wit...'

Dissolving into the next track, 'Women', a subtle, joyous, almost unbearably straight-talking paean to Sylvia and to the whole concept of womanly love, something Lou had never fully embraced since he'd been a boy, wrapped tight in the arms of his former beauty queen mother, Toby. Not that new Lou couldn't still scare the shit out of you: on 'The Gun' he is deadly sincere in his picaresque journey into the mind of a killer. 'I'll put a hole in your face,' he intones, 'Tell the lady to lie down...'

Mostly, though, the songs on *The Blue Mask* deal in the transcendent; those moments when the worst life can offer you coincide with the best. 'The Day John Kennedy Died' is the most obvious example. Another exemplary performance from the band, so cutting yet at the same time so subtle, Lou sleepwalking through a dream that should be a nightmare that it's our job to turn back into a dream, those of us that remain, after it's all dead and gone.

Best of all though is the tumultuous title track, on which the band begins to rage like the four elements all colliding at once as Lou roars his tale of death and salvation as he turns to face the abyss, not as valiant hero, nor brain-damaged saint, but as merely a man, a worthless, puny, self-serving, love-glorifying man. A most thrilling yet disturbing spectacle. Lou called it 'my best album to date. This one's pretty much perfect. It came out the way it was supposed to.' Which was some statement. Yet like the boy who cried wolf the critics remained largely unmoved. All that is, except for the greats, the ones who never feared slipping in the blade whenever they felt it necessary, but who now came out as the reborn Reed's champion. None more so than Robert Christgau, who summed the whole thing up best when he wrote: 'Never has Lou sounded more Ginsbergian, more let-it-all-hang-out than on this, his most controlled, plainspoken, deeply felt, and uninhibited album.'

Even the album sleeve spoke eloquently about the massive change in direction the music was undergoing. Designed by Sylvia, and based, brilliantly, on the old Mick Rock *Transformer* cover shot, but this time overlaid with a blue laminate that gave the cover a dual image: flick the album one way, you got the original Rock shot, turned another you got the blue overlay, signifying the distance Lou had come, and his tacit recognition of that. Even when RCA mucked up the UK printing so that only the original Mick Rock shot was visible, Lou kept his cool. 'I'm bringing all these Lou Reeds together, but the basic image is and has always been – Lou Reed comes from New York and writes rock'n'roll songs.'

Well, yes. And no. There was something more going on here; though, tantalisingly, we would have to wait another decade before that became fully clear. In the meantime, Lou Reed embarked on a sequence of albums throughout the 1980s that stayed true to the line he had taken with *The Blue Mask*, continuing in 1983 with its companion-piece *Legendary Hearts*, which retained the same band, with only one switch on drums, with Fred Maher coming in for Doane Perry. The only real difference was that while the material on *The Blue Mask* had gazed horrified at the world he'd left behind, while basing itself in the new, safer one he was now trying to build with Sylvia, on *Legendary Hearts* he is over the novelty and now coming from a place where he feels free at last to explore the emotional terrain; hence more middle-of-the-frame tracks like the warming title song, or the unashamed takes of domestic commitment like 'Bottoming Out' and 'The Last Shot'. Unfortunately, this could sometimes lead him to rely a little too much on his imagined audience's interest in such things, and tracks like the punk-lite 'Don't Talk To Me About Work' are on the verge of not faintly insulting.

Indeed, by the time we get to *New Sensations*, and it's almost hit single, 'I Love You Suzanne', grown-up Lou sounds like he's actually having *fun*. 'I don't make records for kids or critics,' Lou had told Sandy Robertson at the time of *The Blue Mask*. 'I'm very ambitious. I wanna write my own version of *King Lear* and have it be in a rock'n'roll song...' The songs on *New Sensations*, though, had very little to do with *King Lear*, sounding closer in tone and scope to the listener-friendly cake-and-eat-it happy house of *Coney Island Baby*.

Opening with the rockabilly pop of 'I Love You Suzanne', a hit single for anybody else, a total flop for Lou Reed, *New Sensations* was so listenable that while it wouldn't be rewarded with any gold albums, it attracted the attention of an advertising agency executive, Jim Riswold, then chief copywriter for the Madison Avenue giants Wieden & Kennedy. Riswold would become much better known in the late 1980s for his groundbreaking work with Michael Jordan and Nike, where the ads did more than just try and sell you some trainers but plugged you into a whole lifestyle trip, connecting with the vibe as much as the product. This was fancy stuff for the advertising world of the 1980s and Riswold was at its cutting edge. So he approached Lou Reed to help make an ad for Honda scooters.

At the time, Riswold recalled, 'advertisers didn't put people in commercials who had a long history of drug addiction, and of course [Lou Reed] was a man who at one time in his life was married to a man, and that man was a transvestite, so I guess you could say he wasn't your typical spokesman. But if you looked at who we were trying to sell scooters to, it was natural. Actually, when you look back at that commercial it seems pretty damn tame today.'

Actually, at the time it just seemed plain hilarious. Lou Reed in a TV commercial? Selling scooters? Not least as Lou had used the groove-slinky title track of *New Sensations* to eulogise his now regular road trips on his beloved Kawasaki GPz750 Turbo motorcycle. The kind of monster bike that eats scooters for breakfast then spits out the bones. 'I love that GPz so much,' he croons like a sheep-killing dog, 'that I could *kiss her...*' In the Honda ad though, we get a one-minute jump-cut clip set to the skipping instrumental backdrop of 'Walk On The Wild Side', replete with cut to a heavy-looking street busker laying back on that baritone sax, as the camera then swings round to find Lou perched atop a red scooter, taking off his sunglasses (at night, natch) to tell us: 'Hey, don't settle for walking.' It feels right looking at it now on YouTube that you can 'like', then add a hearty but sincere 'LOL'.

But that was Lou Reed in the 1980s. Shucking it up for the camera and then jumping right back on his GPz, his back pocket tight against his newly engorged wallet. This, after all, was the guy who would one day write in the liner notes of his compilation album *NYC Man*: 'You could have the IQ of a turtle and still play a Lou Reed song' in reference to 'Heroin'.

'It's actually two chords and I'm being funny,' he would say when reminded unkindly perhaps in 2003, long after his 1980s dash for cash and at a time when he was probably now the most seriously treated rock artist on the planet. 'But yeah, the turtle could do a really stupid version of it, but that's like saying that an idiot could say Charlie Malloy's speech in *On The Waterfront*. Any idiot could say: "Charlie, it was you, Charlie. Charlie, it was you, I could have been somebody, Charlie." Anybody could say that. Brando though, that's another story. So it's the way the artist presents it. That's the defining moment.'

One thing *Legendary Hearts* and its equally easy-on-the-ear follow-up in 1986, *Mistrial*, also did for Lou Reed was put him back up the world's charts again. He would never have the big hit he had always secretly craved, his days of wondering why the public preferred, as he saw it, frauds like the Rolling Stones to his own more 'street real' musical mien long over, but he was delighted and not a little relieved nonetheless when *Legendary Hearts* and *Mistrial* at least returned him to the US Top 50, somewhere he had not been allowed to visit since *Coney Island Baby* a long, weird decade before. Along with yet another live album, *Live In Italy* in 1984, a perfunctory release of which seven of its 15 tracks were the usual Velvets standards, with the obvious two from *Transformer* and the obvious two from *Sally Can't Dance*, plus just four from the 1980s, the five-album RCA deal Lou had signed back in 1981 was now at an end. Contract extensions were discussed but Lou felt, rightly for once as it turned out, that it was time for another fresh start.

There was another, deeper reason why Lou Reed now felt the need to stick his head above the parapets again, to abandon the safe new musical home he had built for himself since he'd married Sylvia. It was the death, on 22 February 1987, of Andy Warhol, who at the age of just 48 had somehow failed to survive a 'routine' gallbladder operation at New York Hospital. Lou had not spoken to Andy since their last falling out, during a visit he and Sylvia made to the artist's 'new' Factory at 869 Broadway, right by Union Square where Max's had once been. When Andy had been bitchy to him in front of Sylvia Lou never forgave him. But at the memorial service for his death, held on 1 April 1987 at St Patrick's Cathedral in New York, it hit home to him how much he owed his life and career to the days when he was

Andy's favourite songwriter. At the dinner afterwards, as old Velvets songs wafted underneath the bristling conversation of the gathered Factory tribe, past and present, he found himself talking for the first time in years to John Cale. Billy Name was there too, of course, and it was Billy who suggested to John that he should perhaps compose a memorial piece to Andy. John was taken with the idea and would spend the next few months attempting to do just that, working alone at home in his studio. But he found it near impossible to try and encapsulate the Warhol story in words. He thought about possible collaborators but nobody was brave enough to tackle such a huge subject.

At the same time Lou Reed had also thought to write something for and about Andy, though he did not have the concept of a memorial in his mind as yet. Instead he found himself simply unable to sleep and so would tiptoe into his office and simply type out some of his jumbled thoughts onto the computer. Of course, Lou being Lou, it wasn't long before these thoughts became verses and the verses became... songs? Was that even the right word?

Lou realised he didn't know any more. Certainly they were nothing like the well-crafted burger-and-Cokes he'd spent the last few years putting together with such pleasure for his solo albums. He also found himself writing about other friends he'd lost along the way, other places and times that now had a sharper resonance for him than they ever had before, as if the close proximity of death had shaken him out of a stupor. The late 1980s were the time of AIDS, when the artistic community of New York City – so long driven by the force of its gay frontrunners and creative Catherine wheels

– was being hit by an unstoppable hurricane. Lou Reed had spent so long trying to love down the past, it was only now he realised how close it all still was. He carried on writing, not just songs about Andy any more, but about everything that had been bursting to get out of his head since he finally quit drugs, quit The Life, and started to breathe properly.

That was when he knew that whatever he did next, whatever music he made or people he worked with, there very little time left to lose. When John Cale called him out of the blue in May 1988, to ask him if he'd lend a critical ear to his now completed Andy Warhol memorial piece, Lou was more than ready. When he politely suggested he might put some of the lyrics he'd been writing with Andy specifically in mind to some of the music, Cale was relieved and delighted. All the enmity had suddenly vanished, as the two gathered their forces together again at last, and began to do something meaningful with it. 'There seemed a great need to put the record straight,' said Lou. 'John had already written an instrumental piece for Andy, a mass of sorts. But then the opportunity arose to do the bigger thing...'

10
The Tao of Lou Reed

Lou Reed and John Cale were finishing up their 'mass' for Andy Warhol when, on 18 July 1988, they received a phone call with the news that Nico had also just died, falling off her bicycle and hitting her head on a rock, while on holiday with her son, Ari, in Ibiza. A passing taxi driver had found her unconscious by the side of the road and driven her to hospital, but she had died at eight o'clock that night, of a cerebral haemorrhage. She was 49. The two men took the news in their own different ways. Cale, who had produced the last of her six solo albums, *Camera Obscura*, three years before, was openly distraught. Reed shielded off the shock-waves until he could be alone, to think it through.

Later that night he recalled the last time he had seen her, strung out and begging him for drugs, as he sat there and goaded her like an animal. But that had been in another lifetime, centuries ago, and he preferred to think back to day she asked him: 'Oh, Lou, won't you write a song for me? Nico needs a song, Lou…' in her frozen German accent, and he had responded by writing 'I'll Be Your Mirror', then seethed with jealousy as she sung it so beautifully, so hot and coldly onstage with the Velvets, as if she were the real star of the show, which was of course how Andy always dreamed of it anyway.

Then, before he had time to assimilate what had happened, he received better news. His friend and contemporary Seymour Stein, the Brooklyn-born co-founder of Sire Records – once the new wave label du jour in New York that brought the world The Ramones and Talking Heads, now in the 1980s home-from-home for zillion-selling but still credible artists like The Pretenders, Madonna and Depeche Mode – had made an offer to sign Lou to the company, in exchange for a large cash advance and the promise of top-drawer budgets for whatever albums he chose to make for them.

Leaving his introspective gloom behind, Lou left the niceties of finishing the joint album – now sweetly titled *Songs For Drella*, after Andy's old nickname – to John and began to search around for a producer to record his first all-important album for Seymour and Sire. His previous 1980s albums had credited Lou as producer or co-producer, and that had been fine for what it was. Now, though, determined to make the most of a newly energised Stein, who had promised to pull out all the stops, Lou sought a big name to help him with the project.

Talking to the drummer Fred Maher, whom he'd hired again to play on the sessions, Lou asked him who he thought would make a good producer. Fred ran down a list of the current hot names, including Bob Clearmountain, who'd recently produced platinum hits for Bryan Adams, The Pretenders and Simple Minds, and Scott Litt, fresh off the back of two platinum R.E.M. albums in a row. But according to Maher no one was interested. 'No one.'

In a touching and revealing communication with the music industry guru and internationally acclaimed blogger Bob Lefsetz, in the days that followed Reed's death, Maher recalled how finally he plucked up the courage to suggest he produce the album. Lou glared at him: 'What the fuck do you know about recording guitars? All you've done is synth pop crap', referring to Maher's most recent gig with British electronic collective Scritti Politti. Unabashed, Maher pushed Reed to give him just one day in the studio 'and let's see what happens'.

Desperate to get something going on the album, Lou booked a single day at Media Sound studios on 57th Street. When at the end of it they had the track, 'Romeo Had Juliette', that would eventually open the album, Maher was ecstatic but still left to stew overnight while Lou took the tape home for a long listen. 'He called me the next morning,' Maher would tell Lefsetz, 'and said "I sound like Lou Reed again for the first time in years. Let's do this…" He did not want to change a single thing about it. No remix, no overdubs, nothing.'

Using Leonard Cohen's sparsely recorded *I'm Your Man*, released earlier that year, as his inspiration, Maher was able to fashion a stark yet compelling sound for the album Lou had decided he would call *New York*. When Maher suggested they omit any suggestion of keyboards, Lou went with it. Drawing on some of the songs he'd written in the wake of Warhol's death, though unrelated specifically to Andy, he was determined that *New York* would be his first big musical statement in years.

And so it proved. Featuring a stunning array of cinematic songs, each its own self-contained universe of multi-level stories and ideas, such as 'Halloween Parade', after the annual gay pride march: 'There's a downtown fairy singing out "Proud Mary" as she cruises down Christopher St. / And some southern Queen is acting loud and mean where the docks and the Badlands meet.' Or the au-courant 'Good Evening, Mr Waldheim', a straight attack on Jesse Jackson, who had recently fallen foul of the Jewish community in his presidential election campaign, after making remarks about New York being 'Hymie-town' – which was bad enough, said Lou, 'But to be tied up with [Louis] Farrakhan is intolerable.'

Released in January 1989, *New York* would be lavished with the same kind of unqualified critical praise that Bob Dylan would receive for his 'comeback' albums just a few years later. *Rolling Stone* made *New York* their album of the month, Anthony DeCurtis declaring it 'indisputably the most ambitious album of Lou Reed's solo career... whatever future there is, whenever anyone wants to hear the sound of the Eighties collapsing into the Nineties in the city of dreams, *New York* is where they'll have to go.' As a result, *New York* became the first – and last – Lou Reed album to find the US Top 40. Had the old goat been holding out on us all along? Knowing he could just jump back into mainstream consciousness at will, any old time he wanted? Well, no. But you'd have had a hard time convincing Lou Reed of that as he basked in his reclaimed fame in 1989.

It was around this time I met Lou Reed. Sire was doing everything to push the album just as they'd promised him they would. Sunset Boulevard, where I was then staying, was aflame with posters and billboards for *New York*, the bold black-and-white cover of multiple Lou Reeds posing 20 feet tall across the windows of Tower Records, *the* place to shop for your music in those pre-internet days. Lou was on the promotional treadmill and the Sire publicity department, having covered all the heavy hitters, were now shepherding him through a final round a cherry-picked rock magazines and 'foreign' writers, like me. I didn't get long with him and Lou establishing my credentials took up most of the time. When someone introduced me as the 'go-to guy' for bands like Guns N' Roses and Metallica, he sneered. 'Axl Rose? *Puhlease...*' But I trundled on, babbling about *New York*, relating it back to the beginning of his latest artistic renaissance with *The Blue Mask*, and eventually he let me off the hook. For a second. I no longer have a copy – it was written on a typewriter and the cassette containing the interview probably got left in the same dumper as the typer at some point over the years. But I do remember being surprised when I played the tape back how often I heard myself laughing, at how funny he was in person. And how hilarious so much of his work over the years had been. People – critics – never really got that, I realised, apart from *Take No Prisoners* and even that they approached slowly as if it were a dirty bomb, trying to make sense of it, digging for what it all meant. Like the story of Lou's infamous reaction to the news of Jim Morrison's death: 'He died in the bathtub? *How fabulous...*' People were offended. Always so offended. When really they should have been laughing along with him. At least some of the time anyway...

But that's not how things would be played out. From here until his death almost 25 years later, Lou Reed would release just four more solo albums, plus two collaborative albums and one album of meditative music. Each one taken more and more seriously – that is, until his last, the 2011 collaboration with Metallica, *Lulu*, which almost everybody did laugh at but, as usual, for all the wrong reasons.

In the main, though, this late phase of Lou Reed's career would finally afford him all the critical acclaim and high-brow attention he felt he deserved. Well, nothing would ever come close to giving him what he felt he *deserved*, but gone at least were the caveats and qualifications of the 1980s and the downright contempt he'd been held in for so long in the 1970s. More even than in the 1960s – when, let it not be forgotten, nobody really said much about the Velvet Underground, their place in history only becoming assured posthumously – the Lou Reed who somehow survived into the twenty-first century was a revered figure, a giant of music and art, whose words were listened to carefully now, sifted and treasured, even when he was dishing the dirt on whoever his latest target was. Indeed, the impatient, grumpy old man persona he retained in interview became a feature of his act the same way it did for Bob Dylan or Gore Vidal. Writers would come away disappointed if Lou Reed *didn't* give them the famous limp-dick handshake or sniff at their questions the way a dog does a lamppost he's about to urinate on.

It was a trend begun with *New York*, which was treated like the Second Coming, rather than the fourth or fifth it actually was. But the new seriousness with which Reed's work was now gifted really took off in earnest with the release a year later of his and Cale's posthumous ode to Andy, *Songs For Drella*, a weirdly compelling suite of songs that, like a book, lays out the facts of Andy's life, as played and sung by Lou and John. But while most of the now fawning media attention was directed at Reed's involvement, it was Cale's contributions that were by far the most brilliantly moving. Lou might have been the only singer in the world who could put meaning into almost cringe-inducingly literal lines like 'Bad skin, bad eyes — gay and fatty / People look at you funny...', as in the opening track 'Smalltown'. But it's not until we hear Cale intoning words straight from Warhol's *Diaries*, as in the spellbinding 'A Dream', that we are finally taken to a place of true empathy for the now-lost silver-wigged visionary. 'He was somebody who created himself,' Lou would reflect just weeks before his own death. 'You know, there he was as a balding commercial artist who took himself off to God knows where and reinvented himself as this guy in a leather jacket and a wig.'

But Lou Reed's reputation was also now enshrined in something more than mere image. Warhol's name might have ended up stamped on Coke bottles, but when the newly installed Czechoslovakian president Václav Havel revealed that same year that the 'Velvet Revolution' that had brought him to power was named after the Velvet Underground it was now beyond question: Lou Reed and his songs about junkies, transvestites, murderers and freaks, his obsession with whores and suicides and drugs and ODs, had helped change the world. Inviting Reed over to Prague for a visit, Havel told him how, on a trip to New York in 1967, he'd purchased *White Light/White Heat*, and became so flabbergasted by its contents he made it his mission to turn on friends and other dissident musicians to it. Lou was even more overwhelmed when Václav showed him a book in which he had handwritten Velvets lyrics that would have once resulted in his arrest as a subversive. It was all too much and Lou flew back to New York determined that nobody would ever laugh at his work again. That even he would now treat it with the seriousness his audience deserved.

When, two years later, he released the beautiful *Magic And Loss*, he revealed it as a requiem for two more dearly departed old friends: Doc Pomus, the man who had written so many of the hits Lou had bought as a kid, and Rotten Rita, the opera-and-speed freak who was always known at the Factory as the Mayor. Detailing what Robert Sandall so eloquently described as 'Reed's grim progress from the cancer ward to the crematorium... The song titles – "Sword Of Damocles", "Goodbye Mass", "Cremation", "Gassed And Stoked" – tell it like it horribly is.' Indeed they do. Yet the abiding feeling one is left with after listening to *Magic And Loss* is one of transcendence. The music – tinkling like wind chimes one moment, screaming with outrage the next – is grandiose yet always well-judged. The deadpan vocals are more appropriately still and truer than ever, perfectly suited to convey the simple, hard-to-take truth, as Lou says on 'What's Good': 'Life's good but not fair at all.'

Paradoxically, just as Reed was using his music to address death, his own profile had never been higher. RCA, now under the aegis of BMG, shrewdly chose this moment to release a compilation box set of his years with the label, which retailed for £30, a hefty price tag that reflected the new regard with which that back catalogue, so derided at the time of much of its original release, was now held. To aid this new re-evaluation of Reed's work as a poet-lyricist came the publication of *Between Thought And Expression: Selected Lyrics Of Lou Reed*, a collection that underlined just how well his songs (from *The Velvet Underground & Nico* up to *Songs For Drella*) stand up on the printed page.

The really big reveal though, came, when it was announced later the same year that the Velvet Underground would be reforming for a world tour. Long before the present-day notion of 'classic' rock bands reforming for victory lap tours had become the norm, it seemed hardly believable at the time that the four surviving members of the original Factory-made band – Lou and John and Sterling and Moe – would agree to such a thing. But they did and the subsequent European tour, headlining arenas – something not even Lou had been able to manage as a solo artist – and occasionally opening at stadiums for U2, became one of the big-ticket successes of 1993.

Watching them playing together again from a balcony at Wembley Arena, the sheer thrill of seeing the Velvet Underground live before our naked eyes playing such all-time history-makers as 'Venus In Furs', 'Black Angel's Death Song', even 'The Gift', for crying out loud, eventually paled into a more even grasp that this, of course, despite the metaphorical masks both band and audience were wearing, could never really be the band that lit up the Dom in 1966, or heckled its own audience at Max's Kansas City. Like visiting the ruins of some ancient burial site, it was both fascinating and grim to be there and experience it, but that would never be the same thing as having actually been there back in 1967, poleaxed out of your mind on methedrine and psychedelics, as Gerard cracked his whip and Nico did her statue dance, back when the world was still young, the Factory gates still open to all-comers, even uptight young freaks like Lou Reed, and Andy could genuinely say 'Gee' and 'Wow' to everything that went on around him and actually fucking mean it.

After that the plan had been for a massive Velvet Underground American tour, along with an *MTV Unplugged* album to go with it. But Lou Reed was now far too smart for that. When he turned his back on the idea, all the old resentments came flooding back, as it became clear Lou would be abandoning them – again. There would be one last, limp-wristed hurrah when they were inducted into the Rock And Roll Hall Of Fame in 1996. But by then Sterling Morrison had also died – of non-Hodgkin's lymphoma – and there was an unmistakably belated feel to the whole deal. Cale, ever the fighter, later dismissed the reunion thing as a joke, telling Nick Hasted in the *Independent*: 'It was agreed upon early on that we were to do whatever we wanted, that we were to do new material, rather than go out and be a parody of ourselves,' Cale sighs. 'But then Mo and Sterling decided this and that old song should be done, and it became an exercise in rehabilitating Lou's catalogue. We wasted two good weeks when we could have done anything. And in those two weeks, we managed to help Lou pick his guitar solos. It became so *boring*.'

But by then Lou Reed had other things occupying his mind as his life entered yet another, more forward-thinking phase. The first evidence of this latest evolution came in his

1996 album, *Set The Twilight Reeling*, which apart from one track, 'Finish Line', a personal dedication to his old college buddy Sterling, was the most fun, upbeat, colourful album Lou had released since the mid-1980s. The reason: the relationship he'd begun two years before with American performance artist and musician, Laurie Anderson, to whom at least three songs on *Set The Twilight Reeling* were clearly dedicated.

Best known outside America for her minimalist pop masterpiece 'O Superman', which reached No. 2 in Britain in 1981, Anderson first met Reed in Munich, where they were both taking part in John Zorn's *Kristallnacht* festival, in 1992. Encouraged to try something new, Reed invited Anderson to read something while he and his band provided the musical backdrop.

When they discovered that they did not live far from each other in New York they agreed to meet. But it wasn't until months later, after Anderson finished a tour, that the two finally got back in touch, going to the Audio Engineering Society Convention, a geeks' paradise of electronic equipment and gadgets, a passion they both shared. When the trip turned into an old-fashioned date with dinner, movie and a walk in the park, their fates were sealed.

What began as a friendship grew quickly into a love affair between 'soul mates' with the inevitable effect on Lou's marriage to Sylvia. By the time the divorce was finalised Reed and Anderson had bought a house together in the West Village, which they shared while still keeping on their own separate apartments. At the age of 54, Lou Reed had finally found the perfect-day relationship he'd only ever theorised about and would never have been convinced could be real. Pretty but tomboyish, with short spiked hair and a fierce intelligence, Laurie was almost the perfect identikit partner for someone like Lou, whose sexual preferences had always veered across all available spectrums. What's more, she was an artist, a musician, a performer, someone he could not only speak to on very deep levels about his own work, but who was also a good friend, an animal lover, a laugh. They could go to exhibitions and shows together and know what the other was thinking, even when they didn't agree. Like any involved couple they would also have falling-outs, fights, temporary emotional estrangements.

For the last five of those years they lived together as man and wife. Married in Boulder, Colorado – halfway between where Laurie was in Los Angeles and Lou was in New York – they held the ceremony in the backyard of a friend's house, before Laurie hurried the same night to perform a concert.

It was of course no coincidence that Reed's next album was called *Ecstasy*. Released in 2000, it was, he explained, a conceptual piece looking back at his own marriages and relationships and the paths they had taken him down, which somehow, miraculously, undeservingly perhaps, had led him to Laurie Anderson. Familiar faces like the guitarist Mike Rathke and bassist Fernando Saunders were back in the fold, and Laurie herself played electric violin on 'White Prism', 'Rouge' and 'Rock Minuet'. No longer over-concerned with what he did or didn't include in his studio sound, Lou sounded what he is: free, out there without fear or envy, telling it like it just might be for you too if you can just let... go.

The remainder of his recorded output in the 2000s, however, would be a deliberate move to spend less time documenting his own dreams and nightmares. A happy Lou did not necessarily make for more than one cool album. Instead, his next album, *The Raven*, released in 2003, was a series of extraordinary musical set-pieces inspired by the stories and poems of another old literary hero, Edgar Allan Poe, including dramatically reworked versions of both 'The Bed', from *Berlin*, and, most extraordinary of all, 'Perfect Day', sung by Antony Hegarty, a then unknown Irish-American singer whose haunting and unique voice Reed was responsible for introducing to the wider world, and whose group, The Johnsons, would be awarded the Mercury Music prize for album of the year in 2005. 'When I heard [Antony sing], I knew I was in the presence of an angel,' Reed told one interviewer. It was his guest spot on *The Raven*, and the attendant publicity he received from it, acknowledged Hegarty, that was 'wholly instrumental in me having success. [Lou] advocated for me very intensely, convinced people it was worth listening to me. Basically he was the reason I got signed eventually to Rough Trade and got my record released.'

Indeed, *The Raven* would be an intriguing statement about Reed's past and present, and feature guest appearances from musicians like Ornette Coleman, David Bowie and Laurie Anderson again, as well as the actors Steve Buscemi and Willem Dafoe. It was also interesting to note the inclusion of a 'fire noise' track, 'Fire Music', as if in a nodding glance back towards one of Reed's own most precious old ghost stories, *Metal Machine Music*.

'I wanted to do some one or two minute little electronic pieces for *The Raven*,' he explained at the time, 'and one piece was called 'Fire Music' and it was kind of like a reaction to 9/11, I wanted to see if I could do *Metal Machine* working through real pain and crying. And being in a digital domain doing that caused things that in analogue were so difficult, very, very difficult. I had trouble getting a lot of the stuff I had in my head into a certain number of frames, but working digitally could speed things up. Things that didn't happen in analogue you could do in two seconds, a lot of the stuff, digitally, especially editing, saves you hours, but there are certain things in analogue that you can't do digitally.'

With the exception of the album he released in 2007, an accompaniment to his meditation, *Hudson River Wind Meditations*, an appealing collection of ambient sound and noise I have yet to meet a single person that claims they can actually meditate to, there would be no more grand musical statements in the Lou Reed story until 2011, and the release of his album with Metallica, *Lulu*, the least likely Reed collaboration ever.

The arguments about this deliciously self-regarding project began the moment news of it escaped like bad gas from the manholes of New York City. The arguments only grew more heated once everyone finally heard it. Boohoo, went Lou's army of post-punk disciples. Foul, cried the metal community. Great rock art is always transgressive, of course. How many Lou Reed and Metallica fans would see this as simple rule-breaking though, and how many just plain wrong, was always going to hover over the actual music like a cloud of flies. Yet what we were left with was the best work either side had made in decades. A masterpiece that compelled you to leave your preconceptions at its threshold as it ushered you into its darkly glimmering shadow.

In the years that followed, Lou became more of a curator for his work than an innovator. The highlight of which came in 2007, when long after the party was officially over, he fulfilled his long-ago dream of bringing *Berlin* to life in all its ragged glory on a stage, along with a 30-piece orchestra-band and 12 choristers. The tour was relatively brief but each night was a gala performance. Reed's long-time friend and *Berlin* aficionado, the acclaimed New York artist Julian Schnabel also filmed the concert, which was released on DVD the following year as *Lou Reed's Berlin*. Unlike the mother album's original release, this time round the music and concept received unanimous critical acclaim the world over.

'It was originally meant to be [just] in Brooklyn and at the Sydney Festival, because St Ann's and the Sydney Festival both backed it,' Lou explained at the time. 'So it was just supposed to be those two shows and that was it. We did enjoy the experience and other people seemed to want to see it, so as this was a one-time-only, never-going-to-do-this-again deal, we said yes.'

Schnabel's realisation of the show was particularly spectacular, given the grim nature of the material. 'He's very close to the original album,' said Reed. 'It means a lot to him, as it does to me. Originally he was doing the settings and then we thought he should direct it, and then he brought in his daughter Lola Schnabel who did all of these wonderful montages going on in back of us.'

Interestingly he never allowed the dramatised inserts featuring Emmanuelle Seigner as Caroline to overwhelm the live action on stage.

'Julian's really good and Ellen Kuras, the cinematographer, is really good. It's kind of astonishing. I would see bits and pieces of it, when they were filming, when they would look back at what they'd done that day, but I didn't often have my back to the audience, I was practising my parts, so I never really saw it, but I think the film shows you details that you might miss in the live show.'

When Reed followed that by then bringing a touring version of *Metal Machine Music* to the world, again to similarly ecstatic I-always-said-it-was-good reviews, it marked an even more astonishing turnaround in a career now almost entirely characterised by such unexpected can't-be-done surprises.

Talking about it in 2003, Reed explained: 'Well, Walter Krieger who did the transcription and Rheinhold that got in touch with me saying they wanted to do this, and I said it's impossible. I mean I've been working on doing a sequel for it forever, and it turned into 'Fire Music' from 'The Raven', and I couldn't imagine anyone possibly being able to play it live. But then they sent me an example of it and it was fantastic. I mean, I know that record backwards and forwards, they had the melodies and the harmonics, everything in it, I was astonished by it. So I said okay, and it was performed in Berlin at the Opera Halle and I performed in the third part of it. I suddenly come in on guitar and they disappear and this one mondo guitar replaces all ten of them and then they come in and we all play together. As fantastic and then we went to Venice with it. And then they toured around Europe doing pieces of the whole thing.'

When Ian Fortnam asked him the same year if he would you describe himself as a great romantic, considering the sheer emotional depth of songs like 'Coney Island Baby' and 'Perfect Day', he replied simply: 'I would not describe myself. I would not describe myself.'

What then about he other side of the coin, did he bear more of a resemblance perhaps to the central characters in psychotic songs like 'Kicks' or 'The Blue Mask'?

'It's a complete and total personality. I mean, I like acting. I took acting and directing and film when I was in school, and I liked writing monologues for myself, and different parts to play, and I would bet that that's got something to do with variety going on in there. I mean, if I wanted to do a cowboy song I would write myself a cowboy part. If I wanted to do a Tennessee Williams monologue, there is no one there to stop me, I'm going to try to do that.'

Reed had originally planned to follow *The Raven* with a set of songs inspired by two early twentieth-century plays by the German expressionist Frank Wedekind: *Earth Spirit* and *Pandora's Box*. Both originally published in 1904 and set in Germany, Paris and London in the 1890s, the stories revolve around Lulu, a magnet for the suffocating desires, backhand love and unfettered abuse of all the men, good and bad, who fall upon her. Until, finally, left with 'no real feelings in my soul', as Reed sings it, she meets Jack the Ripper, whose 'love' proves greatest and most fatal of all. Along the way we get river-deep meditations on what W. B. Yeats described as 'the only subjects seriously interesting to an adult' – sex and death. And like all Lou's best work, *Lulu* is nothing if not adult-oriented music.

A genuinely clubbable for-real rock band – as opposed to the expensively hired hands Reed had spent the past 40 years working with – so straight in their musical ambitions it's as if they have a pole up their collective spine, there's never been much kidding around going on in Metallica's best music. What they brought to Reed's latest muse then was pure blissfully un-ironic fire; a fist of fury to replace the limp wrist. It made for an absolutely shattering combination.

Recorded at Metallica's studio in San Francisco over the summer of 2011, the pre-release hype centred on how little afterthought or reworking went on in the studio. Yet what one encountered on first hearing *Lulu* were incredibly manicured soundscapes, layer upon layer of beautiful noise that left you dizzy and unsettled, enchanted and repulsed, wizened. It's not about individual tracks, though there are immediately several stand-outs like the chilling opener 'Brandenburg Gate' ('I would cut my legs and tits off,' intones Lou, cutting straight to the chase) or 'Pumping Blood', whose demented violins hark back to *Street Hassle* before building over several pendulum-like minutes to a full-on Metallica-sized aural assault.

Ultimately, though, *Lulu* is a conceptual work that has to be absorbed as a whole to even begin to traverse its sonic foothills. At 90 minutes-plus this is not exactly an iPod-friendly trip. Unless, maybe, you happen to be horizontal by the time you get to the final track, 'Junior Dad', the final 12 of its skin-peeling 19 minutes taken over by seductive waves of drone that recall John Cale's viola, Nico's harmonium, and the late Cliff Burton's beautiful bass-washes and neo-orchestral effects on the 1986 Metallica instrumental 'Orion'.

Not then the retrograde thrash classic Metallica's more bovine followers might have been hungering for. Nor the kind of fidgety, post-modern punk-poetry Reed's new legion of broadsheet critics would easily assimilate. But, as Metallica's guitarist Kirk Hammett put it to me: 'Something else. A new animal.' Most mainstream critics got it and praised the album. Traditionalist metal critics were outraged though. Yet like all Reed's best work, this was never going to be an album for the 'average' rock fan. Or as Lou snarls in 'The View': 'I want to have you doubting / Every meaning you've amassed'.

When the album was released at the end of October 2011, though, it proved to be the biggest commercial flop of Metallica's career, their first album not to reach the Top 30 in either Britain or America. 'Why is this surprising?' shrugged Lou, who'd forgotten what it was like to give a shit about chart positions. 'An odd collaboration would be Metallica and Cher. Us – that's an obvious collaboration.'

'We were both outsiders,' said Metallica's drummer, Lars Ulrich. 'We both never felt comfortable going down the same path that everyone else was doing. Metallica's always been autonomous, and Lou Reed is the godfather of being an outsider, being autonomous, marching to his own drum, making every project different from the previous one and never feeling like he had a responsibility to anybody other than himself. We shared kinship over that. And we brought him something that he didn't have, or maybe hadn't experienced so much, which in his own words were "energy" and "weight" and "size' and whatever it is that happens when we start playing... We shared a common lack of ability to fit in with our surroundings.'

As far as Lou was concerned, it was simple. *Lulu* was 'The best thing I ever did. And I did it with the best group I could possibly find on the planet. By definition, everybody involved was honest. This has come into the world pure. We pushed as far as we possibly could within the realms of reality.' He might have been talking about any of his best albums.

There had been plans for a Lou Reed–Metallica tour but, like Berlin exactly 40 years before, they were shelved in the face of the unremitting gloom that greeted *Lulu*. However, Reed did set out on his own tour, including several of the tracks from *Lulu* in the new set. When a much-touted appearance in April at the Coachella Music and Arts Festival in California – then the most hip outdoor musical event in the American rock calendar – was cancelled at short notice because, it was announced, Lou Reed was ill, people assumed it was a blip. A heavy cold perhaps? This, though, really would be 'something different'.

It seemed the years of intravenous drug abuse – a self-harming slow torture Lou's body had always defiantly withstood – were finally catching up with him. A victim more than once in his deliriously misspent youth of Hepatitis C – a disease notorious for its high risk of contracting cirrhosis of the liver at a 20-year remove – Reed now found his liver beginning to fail. The usual course of interferon injections given in such cases failed to stem the spread of infection. By the end of 2012, he had liver cancer, made worse by Type 2 diabetes. A born contrarian, Lou did his best to fight back, keeping up his various projects, his photography, his writing and most especially the tai chi which he had begun to practise for two hours a day over the past decade, under the tutelage of Master Mingyur Rinpoche.

When, in May 2013, he was offered a liver transplant at short notice, he didn't think twice. He went, had the op, and returned to the world a few days later with the online message saying he'd never felt so good. The transplant didn't take, however, and by October the doctors had delivered the news that there were no further options for them to explore, and that Lou should make his peace before leaving this world behind at last.

The news came so suddenly, out of the blue, that late-October afternoon in England, at first I refused to believe it, especially when I Googled for information and found there had been a 'Lou Reed is dead' internet hoax doing the rounds just days before. Only weeks before I had witnessed his appearance in London at the *Sunday Times* talk he gave with Mick Rock, to promote the new photographic book they had collaborated on, drawn from those far-out years when Rock was the celebrity snapper par excellence and Reed the is-he-dead-yet rocker, and suitably titled *Transformer*.

I had chuckled knowingly along with everybody else as Lou was shown some of the Phantom-of-Rock pictures Mick took back then and asked for his thoughts. 'I think he was beautiful and he still is,' deadpanned Lou. 'We could do that again now, with different outfits. But I wouldn't do the nails and the make-up now. Too tiring.'

The 'audience' concluded with Lou waxing rhapsodic about the subject that still, it seemed, rather surprisingly, lay dearest to his old heart.

'See, I truly, truly, truly believe in the power of rock. *Real* rock. Not pop rock. Because when you're feeling down or something [with] power rock, *real* rock, three minutes and you're transformed. You feel better, you are stronger. That's really, really true. And it's still true but you need real rock and roll people to do it. Not just a boy band or something. It's all about belief and power of the heart…'

In a touching memorial in her and Lou's local newspaper, the *East Hampton Star*, Laurie wrote the day after her husband's death: 'Lou was a tai chi master and spent his last days here being happy and dazzled by the beauty and power and softness of nature. He died on Sunday morning looking at the trees and doing the famous 21 form of tai chi with just his musician hands moving through the air. Lou was a prince and a fighter and I know his songs of the pain and beauty in the world will fill many people with the incredible joy he felt for life. Long live the beauty that comes down and through and onto all of us.'

There were hundreds of other tributes paid across the world in the days and nights that followed. Tweeted, Facebooked, in print and on TV and radio. Among them, David Bowie referred to Lou as a 'master', while Talking Heads' front man, David Byrne, said: 'His work and that of the Velvets was a big reason I moved to New York and I don't think I'm alone there. We wanted to be in a city that nurtured and fed that kind of talent.'

Didn't we all…

Discography

1970

Lou Reed & the Velvet Underground – *Startrack Vol. 9*, LP, compilation (Netherlands, Polydor, Metro Records)

1971

Lou Reed & the Velvet Underground – *Lou Reed & The Velvet Underground*, LP (UK, MGM Records)

1972

Lou Reed, LP, (UK, RCA Victor) + 21 other versions
Transformer, LP, (UK, RCA Victor) + 85 other versions
'I Can't Stand It', 7″ single (US, RCA Victor) + 1 other version
'Satellite of Love', 7″ single (UK, RCA Victor) + 5 other versions
'Walk And Talk It', 7″ single (UK, RCA Victor)
'Satellite Of Love/Walk And Talk It', 7″ single (US, RCA)
'Vicious/Goodnight Ladies', 7″ single (US, RCA) + 1 other version

'Walk On The Wild Side', 7″ single (UK, RCA Victor) + 11 versions

1973

Berlin, LP (UK, RCA Victor) + 47 other versions

'How Do You Think It Feels/Lady Day', 7″ single (US, RCA Victor) + 6 other versions

The Velvet Underground & Lou Reed – 'I'm Waiting For The Man', 7″ maxi-single (UK, MGM Records) + 2 other versions

'Caroline Says', 7″ single (UK, RCA Victor) + 2 other versions

The Velvet Underground & Lou Reed – 'Sweet Jane', 7″ single (UK, Atlantic) + 5 other versions

Middle Of The Road & Lou Reed – 'Union Silver/Vicious', 7″ single (Italy, RCA)

'Hangin' Round', 7″ single (Japan, RCA)

'Vicious/Satellite Of Love', 7″ single (Netherlands, RCA Victor) + 1 other version

1974

Sally Can't Dance, LP (UK, RCA Victor) + 27 other versions

Rock'n'Roll Animal, LP (UK, RCA Victor) + 41 other versions

'Sweet Jane', 7″ single (UK, RCA Victor) + 6 other versions

'Sally Can't Dance', 7″ single (UK, RCA Victor) + 4 other versions

Lou Reed & the Velvet Underground – *Lou Reed & The Velvet Underground*, LP, compilation (UK, Polydor) + 1 other version

1975

Coney Island Baby, LP (US, RCA Victor) + 26 other versions
Metal Machine Music, LP (US, RCA Victor) + 18 other versions
Lou Reed Live, LP (US, RCA Victor) + 34 other versions
'Walk On The Wild Side', 7″, single (US, RCA) + 5 other versions

1976

Rock And Roll Heart, LP (UK, Arista) + 23 other versions
'Crazy Feeling', 7″ single, promo (US, RCA) + 1 other version
'Charley's Girl', 7″ single, promo (UK, RCA Victor) + 5 other versions
'I Believe In Love', 7″ single, promo (US, Arista) + 1 other version
'Chooser And The Chosen One/Banging On My Drum', 7″ single (France, Arista)
Lou Reed, LP, compilation, box set (France, RCA)

1977

'Creo En El Amour', 7″ single (Spain, Arista)
'Nowhere At All', 7″ single, single-sided, promo (France, RCA Victor)
'Rock And Roll Heart', 7″ single (UK, Arista)
Walk On The Wild Side – The Best Of Lou Reed, LP, compilation (UK, RCA) + 29 other versions

1978

Lou Reed Live – Take No Prisoners, LP (UK, RCA) + 18 other versions

Street Hassle, LP (UK, Arista) + 21 other versions

Lou Reed & the Velvet Underground – 'Street Hassle', 12″ EP (UK, Arista) + 4 other versions

'Walk On The Wild Side', 12″ promo (US, Arista)

New York Superstar, LP, compilation (Germany, RCA) + 3 other versions

Vicious, LP, compilation (UK, RCA) + 1 other version

Grandes Exitos De Lou Reed, LP, compilation (Spain, RCA)

1979

The Bells, LP (UK, Arista) + 21 other versions

'Disco Mystic', 12″ promo (US, Arista) + 1 other version

'City Lights', 7″ promo (US, Arista)

Takeoff – I Can't Stand It, LP, compilation (Germany, RCA)

1980

Growing Up In Public, LP (UK, Arista) + 15 other versions

'Nowhere At All', 7″ EP (Australia, RCA Victor)

'Public Preview Of "Growing Up In Public"', 12″ promo (US, Arista)

'The Power Of Positive Drinking', 7″ single, promo (US, Arista)

Rock And Roll Diary 1967–1980, LP, compilation (UK, Arista) + 11 other versions

New York Superstar Vol. 2, LP, compilation (Italy, RCA Italiana)

Rock Galaxy, LP, compilation (Germany, RCA International)

1982

The Blue Mask, LP (Europe, RCA) + 19 other versions

Lou Reed Interview. A Radio Interview Album In Which Lou Discusses Track By Track The Songs On His RCA Release 'The Blue Mask', LP, promo (US, RCA)
'Women', 12″ maxi-single, promo (France, RCA Victor)
'Underneath The Bottle', 12″ maxi-single, promo (US, RCA)
'The Blue Mask/Walk On The Wild Side', 12″ (Germany, RCA)
'Women/The Blue Mask', 7″ promo (Italy, RCA Victor)
I Can't Stand It, LP, compilation (UK, RCA International) + 2 other versions
Lou Reed & the Velvet Underground – *Lou Reed & The Velvet Underground*, LP, compilation (Italy, Super Star)
Grandes Exitos De Lou Reed, LP, compilation (Spain, RCA) + 1 other version
Wild Child, LP, compilation (US, Pair Records) + 1 other version
RCA Special Radio Series Vol. XVII, LP promo, compilation, limited edition (US, RCA Victor)
Historia De La Musica Rock, LP, compilation (Spain, RCA)

1983
Legendary Hearts, LP (US, RCA Victor) + 19 other versions
'Don't Talk To Me About Work', 7″ single, promo (Spain, RCA)
Scialpi/Lou Reed – 'Rocking Rolling/Legendary Hearts', 7″ single, juke box (Italy, RCA Original Cast)
'Walk On The Wild Side', 7″ EP, limited edition (France, RCA Victor)
'Martial Law', 7″ single, promo (US, RCA)
Sally Can't Dance/I Can't Stand It, LP, compilation (France, RCA) + 1 other version

A Night With Lou Reed, 12″ Laserdisc, single-sided, PAL (UK, Castle Music Pictures) + 1 other version

1984
New Sensations, LP (UK, RCA) + 19 other versions
Live In Italy, LP (UK, RCA) + 14 other versions
'I Love You, Suzanne', 7″ single (UK, RCA Victor) + 8 other versions
'My Red Joystick', 12″ promo (US, RCA) + 5 other versions
'High In The City', 7″ single (Netherlands, RCA)

1985
'September Song', 7″ single (UK, A&M Records) + 4 other versions
Lou Reed/Jenny Burton – 'My Love Is Chemical/People Have Got To Move', 7″ single (US, Atlantic)
'Hot Hips', 12″ single, promo (US, Arista)

1986
Mistrial, LP (Europe, RCA) + 16 other versions
'The Original Wrapper/Video Violence', 12″ single (US, RCA Victor) + 3 other versions
'No Money Down', 7″ single (Europe, RCA) + 6 other versions
Sam Moore & Lou Reed – 'Soul Man', 7″ single (Europe, A&M Records) + 6 other versions
'Video Violence', 12″ single, promo (US, RCA Victor)
City Lights (Classic Performances By Lou Reed), LP, compilation (US, Arista) + 1 other version
He's Got A Rock'n'Roll Heart, cassette, promo, compilation (US, RCA)

Magic Moments With Lou Reed, cassette, compilation (Europe, RCA)

Wanted!, cassette, promo, compilation (Canada, RCA)

1988

Pop Classics, LP, compilation (Netherlands, Eva)

1989

New York, CD, album (Europe, Sire) + 18 other versions

Walk On The Wild Side, CD, 3″ maxi-single (US, BMG) + 1 other version

'Romeo Had Juliette', 7″ single (US, Sire) + 7 other versions

'Dirty Blvd.', 7″ single (UK, Sire) + 8 other versions

'Busload Of Faith', CD, single, promo (US, Sire)

Retro, CD, compilation (UK, RCA) + 5 other versions

A Rock & Roll Life, CD, promo, compilation (US, Sire Records Company)

1990

Lou Reed/John Cale – *Songs For Drella*, CD, album (Europe, Sire, Warner Bros. Records) + 23 other versions

Lou Reed/John Cale – 'Nobody But You/Style It Takes', 7″ single (Germany, Sire Records Company) + 4 other versions

'Power And Glory', CD, maxi-single, promo (US, Sire, Warner Bros. Records)

Lou Reed, LP, compilation (Italy, DeAgnostini)

The New York Album, VHS, PAL (UK, Sire) + 1 other version

1991

Il Grande Rock, CD, compilation (Italy, DeAgnostini)

1992

Magic And Loss, CD, album (Europe, Sire) + 13 versions

'What's Good', 7″ single (UK, Sire, Warner Bros. Records) + 4 versions

'Sword Of Damocles', 7″ single, promo (Spain, WEA)

Between Thought And Expression – The Lou Reed Anthology, CD, compilation, box set (Europe, RCA, BMG) + 3 other versions

Magic And Loss – Live In Concert, VHS, NTSC (UK, Warner Music Vision)

1993

Lou Reed/Nick Cave/Herbert Grönemeyer – 'Why Can't I Be Good/Faraway, So Close!/Chaos, CD, single (Europe, Electrola, EMI) + 1 other version

Lou Reed & Herbert Grönemeyer – 'Why Can't I Be Good/ Chaos', CD, single (Netherlands, EMI)

'Tarbelly And Featherfoot', CD, single, promo (US, Chaos Recordings)

The Very Best Of Lou Reed, LP, compilation (Greece, RCA) + 1 other version

A Retrospective, CD, album, compilation (Europe, RCA, BMG)

1995

Transformer/Berlin, CD, album, compilation (Europe, BMG Music)

Lou Reed & the Velvet Underground – *The Best Of Lou*

Reed & The Velvet Underground, CD, album, compilation (UK, Global Television)

1996

Set The Twilight Reeling, CD, album (Europe, Warner Bros. Records) + 4 other versions

'Hooky Wooky', CD, single, promo (Europe, Warner Bros. Records) + 3 other versions

'Hang On To Your Emotions', CD, single, promo (Germany, Warner Bros. Records)

'Adventurer', CD, single, promo (US, Warner Bros. Records)

'NYC Man', CD, single (Germany, Warner Bros. Records)

'Sex With Your Parents', CD, single, promo (US, Warner Bros. Records)

'Walk On The Wild Side/Satellite Of Love', CD, single (UK, Old Gold)

Different Times – Lou Reed In The 70s, CD, album, compilation (Europe, BMG) + 1 other version

1997

King Biscuit Flower Hour, CD, promo, compilation (US, King Biscuit Flower Hour Radio)

The Masters, CD, compilation (Europe, Eagle Records)

Perfect Day, CD, compilation (UK, Camden)

Lou Reed & Various Artists – 'Perfect Day', 7″ single (UK, Chrysalis) + 9 other versions

1998

Perfect Night Live in London, CD, album (US, Reprise Records) + 3 other versions

'Perfect Day', CD, single, promo (Germany, Reprise Records)

Rock And Roll Heart, VHS, NTSC (US, WinStar Home Entertainment, American Masters)

1999

The Definitive Collection, CD, compilation (US, Arista)

The Very Best Of Lou Reed, CD, compilation (Europe, Camden Deluxe, BMG) + 1 other version

2000

Ecstasy, CD, album (Europe, Reprise Records) + 8 other versions

'Paranoia In The Key Of E', CD, single, promo (Germany, Warner Bros. Records)

'All Tomorrow's Dance Parties', 7″ EP (US, Norton Records)

'Modern Dance', CD, single, promo (Germany, Reprise Records)

The Wild Side CD, album, compilation (Australia, BMG Australia Limited)

Méér Dan Het Beste Van Lou Reed (1972–1986), CD, album, compilation (Belgium, BMG Ariola Belgium NV/SA)

2001

American Poet, CD, album (UK, Burning Airlines) + 6 other versions

'American Poet', 12″ single (UK, Get Back)

Transformer, DVD, PAL (US, Eagle Vision)

2002

'Who Am I (Tripitena's Song)', CD, single, promo (Spain, Reprise Records)

Legendary, CD, album, compilation (Australia, RCA, BMG
  Australia Limited)

2003

Lou Reed, John Cale & Nico – *Le Bataclan '72*, CD, album,
  limited edition (Europe, Alchemy Entertainment) + 4 other
  versions

The Raven, CD, album (UK, Sire, Reprise Records) + 3
  other versions

Vanessa St James & Lou Reed – 'Sunday Morning', CD, maxi-
  single (Europe, Airplane! Records) + 4 other versions

NYC Man (The Ultimate Collection 1967–2003), CD, album,
  compilation, remastered (Europe, BMG) + 4 other versions

The Raven, CD, promo, sampler (US, Sire, Reprise Records)

2004

Animal Serenade, CD, album (UK, Reprise Records, Sire) +
  1 other version

'Satellite Of Love 2004/Walk On The Wild Side', CD, maxi-
  single, enhanced (Europe, BMG) + 8 other versions

Greatest Hits: NYC Man, CD, album, compilation, remastered (Europe, BMG) + 4 other versions

Platinum & Gold Collection, CD, album, compilation (US,
  BMG Heritage)

2005

Spanish Fly – Live In Spain, DVD (UK, Sanctuary Records)
  + 1 other version

Lou Reed Live, DVD, DVD-V, PAL (Germany, Falcon Neue
  Medien)

2006

Collections, CD, album, compilation (Australia, Sony BMG Music Entertainment) + 1 other version

2007

Zeitkratzer and Lou Reed – *Metal Machine Music*, CD, album + DVD, NTSC, Multichannel (US, Asphodel)

Hudson River Wind Meditations, CD, album (US, Sounds True)

The Killers Feat. Lou Reed – 'Tranquilize', CD, single, promo (UK, Vertigo) + 6 other versions

Discover Lou Reed, CD, album, compilation, enhanced file, MP3 (US, RCA, Legacy)

Lou Reed/Transformer, CD, album, compilation (Europe, Sony BMG Music Entertainment)

Lou Reed's Berlin – A Film By Julian Schnabel, DVD + album (US, Artificial Eye)

Walk On The Wild Side, DVD, NTSC (Germany, Veo Star)

2008

Berlin: Live At St. Ann's Warehouse, CD, album (UK, Matador) + 2 other versions

Lou Reed/Laurie Anderson/John Zorn – *The Stone: Issue Three*, CD, album (US, Tzadik)

Lou Reed's Metal Machine Trio – *The Creation Of The Universe,* CD, album, limited edition (US, Sister Ray Recordings)

Original Album Classics, CD, albums, compilation, box set, remastered (Europe, RCA, Sony BMG Music Entertainment, Legacy) + 1 other version

Greatest Hits (Steel Box Collection), CD, album, compilation
   (Europe, Sony BMG Music Entertainment)
Coney Island Baby/Berlin, CD, album, compilation, box set,
   remastered (US, RCA, Legacy, BMG)

2009
Perfect Day: The Best Of Lou Reed, CD, album, compi-
   lation (UK, Camden Deluxe, Sony Music) + 1 other
   version
Lou Reed, CD, album, compilation, DVD, box set, (France,
   fnac.com)
Original Album Classics, CD, albums, compilation, box set
   (Europe, Sony Music, Legacy, RCA)
The Best Of Lou Reed, CD, album, compilation (Europe,
   Camden)

2011
Lou Reed & Metallica – *Lulu*, CD, album (UK, Vertigo) +
   21 other versions
Lou Reed & Metallica – 'The View', CDr, single, promo
   (Japan, Warner Bros. Records) + 1 other version
The Essential Lou Reed, CD, album, compilation (Europe,
   Sony Music, RCA, Legacy)
Original Album Classics, CD, albums, compilation, box set
   (Europe, RCA)

2012
Junkie XL Feat. Lou Reed – 'Going (Demo 2004)', MP3
   (2012, Junkie XL Self-released)

2013

Original Album Series, CD, album, compilation, box set
   (Europe, Rhino Entertainment Company)
Unknown
'Walk On The Wild Side', 7″ single, promo (US, RCA)
'A Rare 1972 Interview With "The Man"', 12″ picture disc,
   limited edition (UK, Baktabak)
Lou Reed/David Bowie/Five Man Electrical Band – 'What's
   It All About?' 7″ single (US, TRAV)
Walk On The Wild Side – His Best 15, LP, compilation
   (Australia, J & B Records)
Lou Reed & the Velvet Underground – *The Best Of Early
   Years* CD, album, compilation (Brazil, Sum Records)

Notes and Sources

The author wishes to offer his utmost thanks to the following writers for their kind permission to quote from their work.

Paul Trynka
Bruce Pollock
Ian Fortnam
Barney Hoskyns
Phil Sutcliffe
Nick Hasted
Charles Shaar Murray
Richard North
Peter Doggett
Also to Lars Ulrich and Kas Mercer for permission to quote from his moving *Guardian* piece on Lou.

Some material was also co-opted from some notable other sources, not least the superb and lengthy 1976 interview for *Melody Maker* by the late great Caroline Coon.

Sandy Robertson, whose wonderful Lou-interview from *Sounds* in 1983 was even better than I remember it. And also for offering insight and much debate about Reed's music and his eventual place in the rock firmament over the years.

Giovanni Dadomo, one of the few British writers who Lou actually dug, and whom I was honoured to have known and learned from.

The late Robert Sandall, whose brilliant voice – in print and on radio – I, like so many others, still so greatly miss.

And of course the late and perpetually legendary Lester Bangs, who not only conducted the greatest Lou Reed interviews ever, but showed the way forward for any rock journalist foolhardy enough to think they could follow him.

Also... Robert Christgau, castigated on *Take No Prisoners* but actually probably the most astute critic of Reed's music ever.

Richard Williams, who, without knowing it, actually helped introduce me to the occult pleasure of the Velvet Underground at a far-too-young age.

Mick Rock, for the never-to-be-repeated pictures, not just of Lou Reed but of David Bowie, Iggy Pop and all the others that made Mick 'the man who photographed the 1970s'. A genuine living legend.

The great Aynsley Dunbar, for kindly sharing his memories of *Berlin*.

Nick de Grunwald, whose superb *Classic Albums* series I was privileged to appear in and help out with occasionally.

There were also some books that proved very helpful. Some of these listed here provided excellent information, all of them provided superb inspiration. Most especially the excellent 1994 Victor Bockris biography, which I am delighted to note he will be updating next year and which I thoroughly recommend. Bockris was the doyenne of the New York music-literature scene in the 70s and 80s, and was giving me great insights and inspiration many years before my own books. Also Peter Doggett, who I have known off and on for nearly 30 years and whose work is always impeccable. Deep thanks to one and all.

Victor Bockris – *Lou Reed* (Vintage)
Peter Doggett – *Growing Up In Public* (Omnibus)
Paul Trynka – *David Bowie: Starman* (Sphere)
Richie Unterberger – *White Light/White Heat: The Velvet Underground Day-By-Day* (Jaw Bone)
Victor Bockris – *Up-Tight: The Velvet Underground Story* (Omnibus)
John Cale – *What's Welsh For Zen* (Bloomsbury)
Michael Wrenn – *Lou Reed: Between The Lines* (Omnibus)
The Velvet Underground: New York Art, edited by Johan Kugelberg (Rizzoli)